LEO TOLSTOY AND THE BAHÁ'Í FAITH

'Abdu'l-Bahá, son of the founder of the Bahá'í Faith and its appointed head during the years of Tolstoy's relationship with this new religion

Leo Tolstoy
and
The Bahá'í Faith

by

LUIGI STENDARDO

Translated from the French by
Jeremy Fox

GEORGE RONALD
OXFORD

GEORGE RONALD, Publisher

British Library Cataloguing in Publication Data

Stendardo, Luigi
   Leo Tolstoy and the Bahá'í Faith.
   1. Tolstoĭ, L. N.—Religion and ethics
   I. Title
   891.73'3   PG3415.R4

   ISBN 0-85398-214-7
   ISBN 0-85398-215-5 Pbk

Contents

List of Illustrations

To my mother and father,
in token of eternal gratitude and affection

Preface

This book is the result of a thesis which completed my studies in Russian in the Faculty of Letters of the University of Geneva. It is a chronological study which treats a little-known aspect of Tolstoy's productive intellectual activity: the famous author's relationship with the Bahá'í Faith.

In gathering the quotations taken from the many works of Tolstoy as well as from the testimony of those who were close to and knew him, I have attempted to ease the burden of future researchers and to familiarise the reader with Tolstoy's thought and religious convictions.

The purpose of this work not being to give an exhaustive presentation on the Bahá'í Faith, I ask the reader to consult other sources listed in the Bibliography.

I wish to express my most profound gratitude to Professors Georges Nivat and Simon Markis, my thesis directors; Miss Jeanine Muller-Dumas for her assistance in its composition; Mr Jeremy Fox for his translation of the work into English, and Mr Albert Ouimet for his speedy and efficient editing. Mr Adib Taherzadeh and Mr Hamid Samandari were invaluable in the translation of Persian texts. All renderings of the quotations into English are by the translator, unless otherwise indicated. I wish equally to thank all those who encouraged me to pursue and to finish this work, particularly Mrs May Ballerio and my wife, Vida.

Luigi Stendardo
Nyon, Switzerland

Introduction

Over the years, few writers have exercised such great and profound influence on their contemporaries as Leo Tolstoy. To the general public, the author's fame is above all due to his novels; but for those better acquainted with his person and writings, there is no doubt that Tolstoy's philosophical and religious ideas are of greater significance than his literary work, to which he himself, in his latter years, only attached slight importance.

The Christian Church considered him a religious heretic. The authorities feared his public pronouncements, often viewed as subversive. Tolstoy was an embarrassment to any form of establishment. Throughout his life, he had searched for religious truth, and he had thus been led to certain conclusions which form the basis of a rationalist faith which he endeavoured to transmit to his contemporaries through his writings and correspondence. In the course of his tireless search for a universal religion, Tolstoy became interested in oriental religions and ideas. His encounter with the Bahá'í Faith occurred in this context and is a relatively-unknown aspect of his life and thought.

1

Tolstoy's Religious Vision

In his introduction to the treatise, *What Is My Faith?*, in which he outlines the evolution of his religious beliefs and which he wrote in 1884 when he was 56 years old, Tolstoy asserts the following:

I have lived 56 years and, with the exception of the last 14 or 15 years of my childhood, I was for 35 years of my life a nihilist in the literal sense of the word – that is to say, I was neither socialist nor revolutionary, in the commonly-accepted sense of the word: to me, nihilism signified the absence of all religion.

Five years ago, I came to believe in the teachings of Christ and suddenly the whole of my life changed: I ceased to wish for that which I had previously wished, and I began to desire things that I had up till then not desired. That which previously seemed to me to be good now seemed bad, and what had seemed bad now seemed good . . .

Like the thief, I knew that my past and present life was evil, and I saw that most men lived like me. Like the thief, I knew that I was unhappy and that I was suffering, that others around me were unhappy and suffering, and the only way out of this situation that I could see was death. Like the thief nailed to his cross, I was attached to this life of suffering by some force. And like him, I saw the approach of the horrible shades of death following the sufferings and evils of a senseless life.

I thus resembled the thief, but there was, however, one difference between us: he was going to die, while I was still alive. The thief facing death hoped perhaps to find salvation beyond the grave, while I still had my life in front of me. I understood nothing about this life.

It seemed terrible to me. But suddenly, I heard the words of Christ and understood them, and then life and death were illumined; instead of despair, I tasted a joy and happiness that death could not destroy.[1]

In these moving terms, Tolstoy comments on the spiritual crisis which marked his life prior to his discovery of the true message of Christ. According to his testimony, this reconversion had occurred five years earlier. However, we could say that the whole of his previous life had been a preparation for this spiritual birth and that its evolution, though long and laborious, had already started in his adolescence and had never been interrupted; all the preceding stages of his life had been valuable and important in the progressive development of his future beliefs.

Tolstoy spent his childhood in a religious atmosphere, marked by several family crises (the death of his mother when he was two years old, and of his father when nine). From his earliest childhood, he was taught the principles and dogmas of the Christian religion as well as the rites and worship of the Orthodox Church. As a child, Tolstoy accepted and assimilated all these principles even though he did not understand them, blindly observing what he was taught, without asking himself any questions. Although from his early youth Tolstoy began to investigate the nature of the mysteries to be found in the Christian Church, he accepted and respected the beliefs which he inherited. Already, when he was twenty-four, the Church doctrines seemed strange and absurd to him, but he told himself that he must be wrong, since millions of Christians could not be mistaken. He noted in his *Diary* for 14 November 1852:

I have composed a short statement of my belief:
I believe in one incomprehensible and benevolent God; I believe in
the immortality of the soul and in eternal retribution for our deeds; I
do not understand the mystery of the Trinity and the birth of the Son
of God, but I respect and do not reject the faith of my forefathers.[2]

Although in his introduction to *What Is My Faith?* Tolstoy
states that he became a nihilist during a certain period of his life,
nevertheless, we cannot say that he was completely atheistic.

Although various other pursuits outweighed his religious
preoccupations, throughout his *Diary* it seems that the concept
of God and the mystery of life and death continued to intrigue
him. On 13 July 1854, he returns to and reaffirms the same
declaration of faith written a few years earlier:

My prayer: I believe in a single, benevolent, all-powerful God, in the
immortality of the soul and in eternal retribution for our deeds; I wish
to believe in the religion of my forefathers, and I respect it.[3]

But, hungry to discover happiness and God, his soul was
slowly tormented by internal conflict. How could he reconcile
the religion of his fathers with reason? The idea of a Christianity divested of all its man-made dogmas and institutions,
which seemed to him contrary to reason, gradually came to
him.

Yesterday, a conversation concerning God and faith led me to a great
idea, a wonderful idea, to the realization of which I feel capable of
devoting my whole life. This idea is the establishment of a new
religion suited to man's level of development, the religion of Christ,
but stripped of the elements of faith and the mysteries, a practical
religion, not promising happiness in a future life, but providing
happiness here on earth. It is quite clear that only several generations
consciously working towards this goal can bring this idea to fruition.
One generation will transmit this idea to the next, and maybe one
day, fanaticism or reason will see it through. To work consciously to
bring man back to religion, such is the basis of the idea which I hope
will occupy my enthusiasm.[4]

1. *The brothers Tolstoy: from left to right – Sergei, Nicholas, Dmitri and Leo*

2. *Tolstoy in the Caucasian army, 1852*

3. *Tolstoy at 32, during his European sojourn*

In this declaration Tolstoy expresses his intention of wanting to devote himself to the establishment of God's Kingdom on earth, and it already indicates the seed of that messianic idea which was to preoccupy him during the latter years of his life.

With his restless and sincere mind, Tolstoy attempted to overcome this religious crisis, this dilemma between Christian doctrine and human reason, by throwing himself into many different activities. He undertook long journeys across Europe. He visited Germany, France, Switzerland and Italy, and investigated their customs, literature and art. In 1862, he married Sophia Andreyevna Bers, a young girl sixteen years his junior. Their first years of marriage were full of happiness. In this state of bliss, Tolstoy undertook the task of writing two great novels - *War and Peace* and *Anna Karenina* - which achieved a resounding success and made the author known and appreciated beyond Russia's boundaries.

Nevertheless, during all these years of feverish and intense literary activity, his worries and torments of a religious and moral nature did not completely disappear. In the mind of this tireless seeker after truth, various ideas concerning Christianity imperceptibly established themselves and matured: over the centuries it must have deviated from the original teaching of its Founder; the religious authorities had imposed a blind and irrational belief on the people; Christ's message must have lost all its force until nothing but the external structure remained, contrary to the New Testament's teaching.

At last, in the years 1878–1879, the author came to a final conclusion. From then on, he was convinced he had found the true meaning of the New Testament. He confirms this in the introduction to *What Is My Faith?*: 'Like the thief, I believed in Christ and I was saved.' But when speaking of Tolstoy's religion, we must not imagine a fixed set of ideas which underwent no change or modification during the last thirty years of his life. After his conversion, Tolstoy never abandoned his search for God and true religion.

As we can perceive throughout Tolstoy's religious works, his concept of God is not the same as that of orthodox Christianity. According to him, the Trinity is a purely human invention, there being no such thing as a God who is at one and the same time Father, Son and Holy Ghost. For the author, God is Spirit, Love and the Principle of all things. In his treatise *The True Life* Tolstoy explains his concept of God in these terms:

At a certain stage of his development, man could believe that God had created the world 6,000 years ago, that the earth was the centre of the universe, that hell was beneath the earth, that God had come down to earth and then gone back up to heaven, and so on. But a time came when man could no longer believe in such things because he knew perfectly well that the world is not 6,000 years old, that the earth is not the centre of the universe, but is quite a small planet compared with the heavenly bodies, that there is nothing beneath the earth because it is a globe. Finally, we learnt that it is impossible to go up to heaven because there isn't one, just our illusion of a canopy of heaven . . . [5]

According to ancient beliefs, man, in order to experience God, was required to believe what others told him: how He had created the world and humanity, and had subsequently revealed Himself; while Christian doctrine enables us to experience God directly, by means of our consciousness alone.

Our consciousness tells us that at the heart of our life is a desire for the common good, that this is something inexplicable, inexpressible and at the same time most intimate and palpable. The desire for happiness first became manifest in man at the animal and personal level; then, it extended to those he loved, and finally, with the awakening of his consciousness, to the whole human race. This latter desire is the Principle of all life, or as the Gospels express it, God is Love. But, apart from this awareness of God within himself, man, according to Christian teachings, recognizes God outside himself, in everything that exists. Being aware of God's spiritual and indivisible

Being within his own physical person, and perceiving this same God's presence within all that lives, man must inevitably ask himself why God, being spiritual, single and indivisible, has confined Himself within separate bodies? Why did a unique and spiritual Being become divided within Himself? Why did the Divine Essence confine Itself within definite bodily limits? Why did the immortal principle confine Himself within the mortal principle? Why are they connected? There can only be one answer: there exists a superior will whose purposes remain inscrutable to us. It is this that established the present state of things. This is the First Cause, God, which man senses within himself and recognizes outside himself.[6]

Thus, for Tolstoy, God is Love and the Superior Will whose purposes are inscrutable. This vision of God as single and indivisible is in flagrant contrast with the traditional Christian concept.

Another point of fundamental divergence is the divinity of Christ. Tolstoy considers Jesus Christ not as God come down to earth, but simply as a man more receptive than others to the divine will, as a great soul who taught man the true meaning of life and its goal.

By means of careful study of the New Testament, Tolstoy discovered that the whole of Christ's teachings could be summed up in five basic laws:

1. Do not get angry;
2. Do not commit adultery;
3. Do not swear oaths;
4. Do not return evil for evil;
5. Be no one's enemy.

This was the negative side of the New Testament message. The positive side consisted on the other hand of a single commandment: 'Love your neighbour as yourself.'

The practical consequences resulting from these five

commandments were as follows: prohibition against serving in the law-courts; passive acceptance of all violence; refusal to serve in the army or under the orders of any government, given that all governments use violence to maintain themselves in power. By these attitudes Tolstoy became a heretic in the eyes of the Church, and in the eyes of the authorities an instigator of non-obedience to the laws of the country.

Supported by many proofs (for which he had studied ancient Greek and Hebrew), Tolstoy, in his book *What Is My Faith?* refutes all the 'fantastic' stories told about Christ: the miracles, the Resurrection and His Divinity.

In the book entitled *The True Life* Tolstoy openly attacks the Church and demonstrates that it constitutes the main obstacle preventing man from practising Christ's teachings.

In Chapter XXXV, entitled 'The Procedures of False Religion', the author remarks that false religion uses certain procedures in order to keep man in error. These procedures are of course used by the Christian religion, but also by the other old religions which, like Christianity, have lost the true teachings of their Founder, among others, the teachings of Buddha, Lao-Tse, Zoroaster and Muḥammad. This passage shows us that, at the time of this book's composition in 1901, Tolstoy knew and was already quite deeply interested in other religions, although for the time being, Christ's message still remained at the root of his beliefs.

The interest of this chapter also resides in its minute analysis of the procedures used by all these religions corrupted over the ages by human interpretation:

Truth has no need to be confirmed by example, it is freely accepted by all those who understand it; falsehood, on the contrary, requires special procedures to force us to submit to and accept it.
These procedures applied to faith are the same among all peoples.

There are five of them:
1. False interpretation of the truth;
2. Belief in the miraculous;
3. The creation of intermediaries between man and God;
4. Action on the senses;
5. Teaching children erroneous faith.

The first procedure consists in recognizing, in theory, not only the correctness of the truths revealed by the most recent prophets, but in addition, regarding the prophets themselves as sacred, divine; all sorts of miracles are attributed to them, yet so as to hide the true meaning of the newly-revealed truth, so that it cannot interfere with the old way of life, and even sanctions it. This false interpretation of the truth and divinization of its Founder occur with every people, each time a new religious teaching has appeared. Such was the effect of the teaching of Moses and the Jewish prophets. It was precisely the lying interpretation of Jewish teachings by the Pharisees to which Christ objected, in telling them that they occupied Moses' seat without having entered the Kingdom of God or letting others enter. The teachings of Buddha, Lao-Tse, Zoroaster and Muḥammad met the same fate. Finally, the Christian Faith began to lose its true meaning at the time of Constantine's conversion, when the gods and pagan temples were Christianized, and Islám appeared as a reaction to the supposed plurality of Christian gods . . .[7]

According to Tolstoy, the second procedure consists in persuading man that the knowledge of truth through reason is a sin of pride. The Church teaches that there exists a surer means of acquiring knowledge, that of belief in a direct revelation of truth by God to a few of his elect, a revelation which is always accompanied by visions, miracles or extraordinary events. In short, we are asked to believe not in reason but in miracles, that is to say, in that which is contrary to reason.

The third procedure consists in making man understand that he cannot enter into direct contact with God and that he therefore has need of intermediaries: the church, priests, saints, hermits, dervishes, lamas, Buddhist priests, etc.

The fourth procedure consists in impressing the faithful with the beauty and majesty of temples, the magnificence of the decoration of the accessories of worship, the sonority of singing and the organ, the odour of incense, etc., and while men remain under the influence of this seduction, they endeavour to imbue them with lies.

The fifth procedure, which consists in inculcating the outmoded ideas of generations who lived thousands of years ago, is the most cruel, according to Tolstoy.

To the child who asks his father or teacher what is the meaning of life and how he should behave in relation to his fellow men, they reply by avoiding the question:

If the father is Jewish, he tells him that God created the world in six days and revealed all truth to Moses by writing on stone with His finger. He says that one must observe the commandments, keep the day of the Sabbath holy, be circumcised, etc.; if he is Christian, orthodox, catholic or protestant, he says that Christ is the second person of the Trinity, that he came down to earth to redeem the sins of Adam by his blood, and so on; if he's Buddhist, he maintains that Buddha flew off into heaven after teaching man about the renunciation of life; if he is Muslim, that Muḥammad went to the seventh heaven and brought back the law according to which belief consists in the prayer to be recited five times a day and that the pilgrimage to Mecca gives access to paradise.

Knowing full well that others inspire their children by means of other superstitions, parents and teachers each teach their own, while remaining basically aware that they are but superstitions, and they teach innocent and trusting beings at an age when impressions are so strong that they can never again be erased.[8]

Thus Tolstoy, by means of these words of great clarity and exceptional gravity, through the accusations brought against all ecclesiastical institutions, completely set himself outside Christian society. His excommunication, which dates from that same year (1901), came therefore as no surprise to him: he had already of his own free will departed from the path of orthodoxy and official Christianity. On the contrary, his excommunication provided him with a splendid opportunity to officially express his profound convictions. His *Reply to the Synod* provoked an enormous sensation in Russia; it created many problems for him with the all-powerful clergy, but at the same time, it drew to him the sympathies of thousands of people within the country, in Europe and also in the non-Christian world.

In a clear and concise manner, the *Reply to the Synod* contains Tolstoy's religious ideas; it is very important, if not fundamental, to an understanding of his true beliefs. Indeed, in a single page, the author sets out the essentials of his faith, which in many cases are to be found scattered throughout the vast canvas of his other works. Here then is the crucial passage of Tolstoy's credo:

I believe in God who for me represents the Spirit, Love, the Principle behind all things. I believe He is in me, as I am in Him. I believe that God's will has never been more clearly and precisely expressed than in the teachings of the man Christ, but one cannot consider Christ as God and address prayers to him, without committing, in my opinion, the greatest of sacrileges. I believe that true happiness for man consists in fulfilling God's will; I believe that God's will is that every man should love his fellow-man and always act towards others as he would like them to act towards him . . . I believe that the meaning of life for each one of us is simply to increase the love within oneself; I believe that this development of our ability to love will gain us, in this life, a happiness which will grow each day, and in the next, a happiness all the more perfect because we will have learnt to love more; I also believe that this increase in love will, more than any other force, contribute to the establishment on earth of the Kingdom of God, that is to say, the replacement of an organization of life in which division, falsehood and violence are all-powerful, by a new order in which harmony, truth and brotherhood will reign. I believe that to progress in love, we have but one means: prayer. Not public prayer, in the temples, of which Christ specifically disapproved (Matthew VI, 5–13), but prayer such as he himself gave us an example, which consisted in reestablishing and reaffirming in us the awareness of the meaning of our life and the feeling that we are dependent on God's will alone.[9]

Many works have devoted themselves to the development of Tolstoy's religious ideas. I will cite here two books written in French, *La Vie de Tolstoï* (The Life of Tolstoy)[10] by his contemporary, Romain Rolland, and more recently, Nicolas Weisbein's booklet, entitled *Tolstoï*.[11]

We have seen in a chapter of *The True Life* that Tolstoy seemed to have a good knowledge of oriental religions, and that may be explained by several factors. First, the writer had acquired a certain fame throughout the world and consequently, an ever-increasing host of people were maintaining a more or less regular correspondence with him, and amongst them were people from the orient. People wrote to him from the remotest parts of the globe: from Persia, Egypt, China, Japan and India. This correspondence was very fruitful for Tolstoy, for in this way he gradually became familiar with oriental ideas and religions. In addition, the writer himself had an enquiring mind; he had read the holy books of all religions, as we may observe in his correspondence and his *Diary*. On 20 February 1900, in the *Diary*, he notes: 'I have read the Buddhist sutras; very good.'[12] In addition, Tolstoy introduced several quotations drawn from Buddhism into the compilation *For Every Day*.[13]

Brahmanism also interested Tolstoy, and he maintained a regular correspondence with the Indian religious author Baba Bharaty, who had sent him his book, *Shree Krishna: The Lord of Love*, as he confirms in a letter addressed to Naum Osipovič Ejngom, an Armenian captain in the Russian army: 'I don't have the book on Rama-Krishna Abhedäanda, but I have read a book about him by Baba Bharaty, in which the Krishna legend is very well expounded and includes extracts of his teachings.'[14]

As for Islám, Tolstoy had already had occasion to make its acquaintance in his youth during his stay in the Caucasus, a region where even today a large part of the population is Muslim.

Over the years, Tolstoy's attitude towards oriental religions had evolved: in his youth, he had considered them as every Christian who has been told since birth that Christianity is the only true religion and that the others are false; but little by little, Tolstoy reached the conclusion that Christ's revelation was not unique, that there had been others before Him and since, as he explains in the preface to *The True Life*:

I perceived that it [the solution] in no way results from my personal interpretation of the Gospels, nor even from the exclusive revelation emanating from Christ, but that it is the answer to the question of life, given more or less precisely by the best of men before and since the Gospels: Moses, Isaiah, Confucius, the ancient Greeks, Buddha, Socrates, up to Pascal, Fichte, Feuerbach and whoever thought and spoke sincerely about the meaning of life and who did not adopt religious doctrines with blind confidence.[15]

But, as in the case of Christianity, Tolstoy was also disappointed by the other religions, each one of which attributed to itself an exclusive claim to truth, while at the same time rejecting all others. In this preface, after explaining that the main reason which prevented him from accepting Christianity was the simultaneous existence of different churches – Orthodox, Catholic, Lutheran, Anglican – each one of which claimed to be the only true one, the author observes: 'I also knew that besides Christianity, there existed other religions, Buddhism, Brahmanism, Islám, Confucianism, etc., which likewise considered themselves to be the only true one, and all others as mistaken.'[16]

2

Tolstoy and the Bábí Faith

His inner dissatisfaction, his natural curiosity about all that was new, and the attraction that oriental religions exercised over him, led Tolstoy to become interested in a religious movement which arose in Persia around the middle of the nineteenth century, namely the Bábí Faith. This movement laid the foundations for a religious renewal heralding the birth of the Bahá'í Revelation, now known throughout the world as the Bahá'í Faith. In Tolstoy's time, ignorance of this in the West resulted in the fact that not only were the names Bábí and Bahá'í confused, but also the central figures of these religions were often not distinguished from one another.

Tolstoy manifested an increasing interest first of all in the Bábí Faith, and subsequently in the Bahá'í Faith, either because he often found his ideas in agreement with the basic principles of this belief, or because he was fascinated by the dramatic story of its early history.

On 17 September 1894, Tolstoy mentions the Bábí Faith, of which he had probably heard previously. On that day, the author notes in his *Diary*: 'Yesterday, I wrote a little . . . This evening, I read some letters and articles come by post. Nothing particularly interesting. From Lebedova. About the Bábís.'[1]

On 5 September of the same year, Olga Sergeyevna Lebedova, Tolstoy's translator into Turkish, had sent him a little notebook which contained a translation of an article about the Bábí Faith, and a pamphlet by A. Tumansky, on the same subject. These are the first things we know concerning the relationship between Tolstoy and the Bábí Faith. He had perhaps already read an account of the Báb's life, as seems to be suggested by his reply dated 22 September 1894; but we have no confirmation of this in his previous correspondence:

> Thank you very much, dear Olga Sergeyevna, for sending me the notebook and pamphlet. I read them with interest, but I did not find in them the most important aspect: an explanation of the moral and social teachings (of the Báb). I think that in the Báb's own books these teachings are lost in his verbosity and typically oriental high-flown style, and that the similarity with the Qur'án is very approximate. For this reason, it would be interesting to extract from these books everything which is essential and concerns morality and social life. It would also be interesting to have information about the lives of the Bábís and the practical application of their teachings. If these exist in the English books which you mentioned and, if you have them *and you could spare them*[2] for a while, then I would be most grateful if you could send them to me. I will take care to return them to you punctually . . .[3]

We do not know if Tolstoy received the information for which he asked Lebedova, but this letter is of great interest as it marks the start of the attention Tolstoy gave to the Bábí Faith.

What is the Bábí Faith? Here is an outline of the main features of the Báb's life, martyrdom and teachings.

Mírzá 'Alí-Muḥammad, who subsequently adopted the title the Báb (the Gate), was born in Shíráz, in Persia, on 20 October 1819. He was a Siyyid, which is to say, a descendant of the Prophet Muḥammad. In his earliest childhood, he lost his father and was entrusted to a maternal uncle. As an adolescent, he was renowned for his very handsome appearance, his charming manners, exceptional piety and great nobility of character. He married at the age of twenty-two and had a son who died while very young.

On 23 May 1844 in his twenty-fifth year he declared his mission as the one chosen by God to prepare the way for a Divine Manifestation, for a great one who would establish on a new foundation and new principles an era of peace and prosperity, the Kingdom of God on earth which believers in all religions were awaiting.

His fame and teachings spread very rapidly throughout the whole country, and the all-powerful Muslim clergy tried by every means to prevent the spread of the Bábí movement. Intimidation and persecution became widespread. Thousands of people were beheaded, hung, burnt or cut to pieces. The Báb himself was imprisoned and shot in Tabríz, a town situated in the north of Iran.

In spite of repression, the movement progressed. Then came the great persecutions following the Báb's martyrdom. All those who were considered his followers or sympathizers were imprisoned, tortured or executed. These persecutions became even more intense following an abortive attempt on the Sháh's life by two Bábís, distraught by the martyrdom of their beloved Master, and contrary to the commands for forgiveness and tolerance enjoined by the Báb himself. The echo of these atrocities travelled as far as Europe, and several newspapers of the time reported these events.

In Geneva, two newspapers, *La Revue de Genève* (The Review of Geneva) and the *Journal de Genève* (The Journal of Geneva) in 1852 give an account of these tragic events. Given the international readership these two publications enjoyed, it seems interesting to quote at this point a few extracts.

The *Revue de Genève* of Thursday, 4 November 1852, relates the following:

Yesterday we mentioned the execution of 400 members of the Bábí sect. The *Journal de Constantinople* of the 14th gives the following details on this subject: 'Letters from Tauris (Tabríz), dated 27 September, which arrived yesterday from Trebizond, brought to this town news from Persia, which are of a rather serious nature. Without assuming any responsibility, we cannot pass by in silence what these correspondents announce. The execution in Ṭihrán of about 400 Bábís said to be accomplices in the attempt on the life of the Sháh of Persia, which we reported in our previous issues, took place with a formidable display. They were subjected to the most terrible tortures, and we are assured that the Sháh of Persia is seriously disturbed by the attempt on his life by the Bábís.'

And on Wednesday, 10 November of the same year, we read the following:

Recent letters from Tehran (1 October) give horrific details of the executions which have just taken place in this town . . . It is true that, the number of victims was not as great as first reports announced. Only thirty-two Bábís fell into the hands of the law, following the investigation carried out by two high state officials.

The accused were summoned, and after a short interrogation, six of them against whom there was insufficient evidence were condemned to the galleys for life. The death sentence was pronounced for all the others. The details relating to the execution of these unfortunate people revolt the imagination, and although published in detail by the official government newspaper, a European pen could not bear to relate them. The accused were literally crushed, massacred, skinned alive, cut to pieces. Princes, grand dignitaries, ministers, clergy, generals, down to people occupying the lowest positions and the dregs of society, everybody without exception was required to play an active rôle in this butchery and to dip his hands in blood. The corpses of these unfortunate people were reduced to shreds with unbelievable ferocity, with sabres, axes, spears, hammers, stones, etc. The limbs and pieces of flesh of the principal Bábís were suspended at the gates of the town.

A paragraph in the *Journal de Genève*, dated Saturday, 11 December 1852, relates the following:

The two officers who had entered the service of the <u>Sh</u>áh of Persia, the infantry Captain de Goumoëns (from Vaud) and Engineer Captain Zatti, have left Persia and have set out for Europe. The atrocities committed against the Bábís and other occasions of a like nature have probably given them an aversion to service with the <u>Sh</u>áh.

More than twenty thousand Bábís sacrificed their lives during this period so as not to deny their faith; further information concerning these events may be found in Shoghi Effendi's book *God Passes By*.[4]

The Báb's teachings were very simple. He proclaimed the unity and truth of all the great religions, enjoined upon his disciples to break with past rites and ways of worship and to live in harmony with men of all beliefs, and prepared them for the coming of a further Messenger of God.

These humanitarian principles, which had many points in common with Tolstoy's ideas, could not leave the writer indifferent.

For five years, from 1894 to 1899, we find no further reference to the Bábí Faith in Tolstoy's correspondence, but through an event which occurred during the year 1899 we know that Tolstoy was still seeking out with interest information about it.

That year, at the end of April, three people well-known in the world of European literature visited Tolstoy. They were the German-speaking poet Rainer Maria Rilke,[5] the orientalist Friedrich Carl Andreas[6] and his wife, Lou Andreas-Salomé.[7] During their stay in Moscow where Tolstoy was at that time, the three writers had noted Tolstoy's interest in the Bábí Faith, and Rainer Maria Rilke, upon his return to Germany, wrote him the following letter:

Most honoured Count,

Already on that memorable evening in Moscow, when we three,

Madame Lou Andreas-Salomé, Dr. F. Andreas and I received a profound impression of your personality, an impression which united us in a profound feeling, we conceived the wish to return to see you by means of a book, in order to further maintain this contact which your kindness so simply and admirably created. At that time, most honoured Count, you were interested in the Bábís. Therefore, we are sending you a pamphlet on this subject which we had mentioned at the time of our meeting; Madame Lou Andreas-Salomé has included her most recent book and I, a little book resulting from my vague feelings binding me to my Slav origins in Prague. Thus, most honoured Count, we once more enter your home, one by one, and your great kindness need not extend to our peaceable and patient works with the same alacrity you manifested on the occasion of that belated visit by three strangers united by a profound and sincere respect for yourself, a respect which we once more confirm.[8]

Tolstoy replied to the celebrated Austrian poet with a letter of thanks, dated 25 September 1899:

Dear Sir,

I have received the books of Madame Lou Andreas-Salomé, the book concerning the Bábís and your own. I have not yet had the time to read it, having only read the first three stories by Madame Lou Andreas, which I very much liked. I will not fail to read the others, and I thank you for the books and your letter. I remember with pleasure the agreeable and interesting conversation we had with you and your friends on the occasion of your visit to my home in Moscow.[9]

We have no further news of Tolstoy having read or commented on Andreas' book. Two years later, a Persian prince whom Tolstoy calls Mírzá Rídá Khán and whose real family name was Rídá Arfa'u'd-Dawlih, sent Tolstoy a poem he had composed, entitled 'Peace'. The prince, who was Persian Ambassador in St Petersburg, had also been his country's representative at the World Peace Conference held in The Hague, on 6 May 1899, on Russia's suggestion. Tolstoy had, at the time, criticized the conference, describing it as an example of Christian hypocrisy.[10] Prince Arfa'u'd-Dawlih, when he retired, settled in Monte Carlo. After his death, his house became a museum, now called 'Isfahan', where the original of the letter Tolstoy wrote to him is kept.

Tolstoy answered the prince by explaining to him the essential points of his philosophy. He envisages the adoption by the whole of humanity of a religion based on reason, which is common to all peoples, and finally reminds him that in Persia the Bábís profess the true religion, and that one day they will triumph over the barbarity and savagery of governments. The letter is dated 10/23 July 1901:

My Prince,

I am most grateful to you for sending me your poem. It is most interesting and I believe that the propagation of the ideas it contains will be of the greatest use, not only to the Persian people, but to men on all continents. I absolutely agree with the idea expressed by the last speaker – the Oriental – that in order to cure an evil, one must find the cause and try to suppress it. The Oriental says that the cause of evil is selfishness and ignorance. I would only wish to add to the word ignorance – ignorance of the true religion. By the term true religion, I mean religion comprehensible to all men, founded on that reason common to all peoples and, because of that, binding on all. The basic principle of this religion is expressed in the Gospels by these words: 'Do unto others as you would have them do unto you. This is the Law and the Prophets.'

If only this principle were recognized as the only religious principle for all men, then the selfishness whereby the individual is ready to sacrifice the good of his neighbour in order to attain his own ends, would disappear of its own accord. It follows that I consider ignorance of true religion as the sole cause of evil in general, and wars in particular. I am also not entirely in agreement with you about the brotherhood which you suppose to be possible between states and their leaders. I believe that the State, always formed and maintained through violence, not only excludes brotherhood, but is quite the opposite of it. If men are brothers, there can neither be Emperor, Minister, General, subject nor soldier. Between brothers, no one can have the right to give orders, nor anybody be required to obey. All should obey God, and not men whose orders are most frequently contrary to God's Laws.

According to me, wars will only finish when every individual is so imbued with the religious principle as not to do to others what he would not like done to himself, when no one will be able to accept the obligation of military service which is nothing more than preparation for murder, the act which is most contrary to the principle of reciprocity, since each man clings to life more than to anything else, and consequently, to wish to deprive him of it is to do to others as you would not wish to be done to you.

I believe that everywhere, like the Bábís in your homeland, Persia, there are people who profess the true religion and that, despite the persecutions to which they are always and everywhere subjected, their ideas will increasingly spread and triumph in the end over the barbarity and ferocity of governments, and especially, over the deceit by means of which they try to subject their peoples . . .[11]

In the last part of the letter, Tolstoy maintains once again that wars will be overcome when true religion has been established on earth, and when men refuse to submit to military service.

3

Tolstoy and the Bahá'í Faith: First Contacts

It was during that same year of 1901 that Tolstoy heard for the first time the name 'Bahá'í'. It was also the first time that a Bahá'í established contact with him. This was Gabriel Sacy, a Frenchman of Syrian origin, who, having first been converted from Islám to Christianity, had then become acquainted with the Bahá'í Faith and enthusiastically embraced it. This man, having read in the newspapers in Cairo, where he was living, information concerning Tolstoy's teachings, had decided to write to him to share with him his own religious convictions. His letter, dated 13 May 1901, is reproduced in Paul Biryukov's book, *Tolstoï und der Orient*:

Dear Count,

The person who takes the liberty of writing this letter to you is neither a scholar nor otherwise remarkable. He is but a simple Bahá'í who, upon reading your statement of belief in the Arab newspapers of this country, has come to the following thoughts, and who, knowing the great kindness of Your Excellency, takes the liberty of submitting them to your judgement. The Divine Essence is in itself impossible to define or describe. It infinitely surpasses the most exalted ideas which Jesus himself was able to conceive, who nevertheless represents a very important Manifestation of the Divine Essence, destined to lead humanity towards progress. It is clear that the world without a physician will make less and less progress; every association needs a chairman to direct it – why should not humanity need an educator? Abraham was one for his family, Moses for his people, Christ for many peoples, and so on. All these Prophets together form a single unit, each one is at once distinct and at the same time he is not. The word of the Educator is the Holy Spirit, light, life. To turn away from this Word signifies to fall into darkness, to descend to hell, to advance in the storm without a guide. The blasphemy against the Holy Spirit is worse than that against God the Father and the Son, for the Divine Essence is beyond our comprehension. The Divine Essence is for us, or rather for those who blaspheme against It, unknown. On the other hand, the Holy Spirit gives us life through His Writings and His Word. The Educator attributes to the Divine Essence which inspires Him, names such as God, Love, Creator, etc., and these are the names which the Educator deserves Himself because He creates them. Did not Jesus Christ create Christianity through His Word? Therefore He is the creator. Did He not create it without human knowledge, without an army and without money, struggling against the whole world? He is therefore all-powerful. Did He not sacrifice Himself in order to create it? Therefore He is God, because only God can do this. Through His words, we recognize the One who pronounced them. Even if Christ is God, we prefer not to name Him so because He did not give Himself that name. We call Him the Son of God because He gave Himself that title. His Kingdom, unlike His Father's, is Christianity. 'Our Father which art in heaven, Thy kingdom come. . . ' If only we could dwell there! Whatever we have done in the past, apart from superficial actions, has an influence, either positive or negative, on our salvation. If Your Excellency finds these ideas worthy of further investigation, there are many Bahá'ís in 'Ishqábád, but also in Paris and elsewhere, capable of developing them with greater authority. To close, if you wish to attain the essence of reality, pray to God, the living, all-powerful God, and you will find peace for your soul. That is what your devoted servant wishes for Your Excellency.[1]

Gabriel Sacy

Tolstoy's only known letter to Gabriel Sacy is dated 10 August 1901:

Sir,

I very much regret that I did not receive the registered letter which you mention in your most recent one. I couldn't have forgotten it, to judge by the interest which your concept of messianism inspires in me, as well as Bábísm to which you belong. What is Bahá'í? And what nationality are you? If you are French, how is it that you are a Bábí? Bábísm has interested me for a long time. I have read everything I could on this subject and, although the basic book – Bábísm's bible – seemed to me a book of little value, I nevertheless believe that, from the point of view of its moral and humanitarian teachings, Bábísm has a great future in the oriental world, having much in common with Christian anarchy, and that sooner or later they are destined to join forces. Please accept, Sir, the assurance of my warmest regards.[2]

Tolstoy's reaction is interesting for three reasons: first, the writer has never heard of the Bahá'í Faith before, because he asks Gabriel Sacy, 'What is Bahá'í?'; secondly, Tolstoy is still convinced that the Bábí Faith is a religious movement limited to the East, and is very astonished that a Frenchman, a westerner, should belong to it; thirdly, to his correspondent who states that he is a Bahá'í, Tolstoy writes: 'How is it that you are a Bábí?' This indicates a confusion in the author's mind over these two terms. Tolstoy had probably not understood the relationship existing between the Bábí and Bahá'í Faiths.

Sometimes, and one can see this throughout his letters, the author seems to make no distinction between 'Bábísm' and 'Bahá'ísm', and alternates between the two words, while elsewhere he prefers to use just one of them.

If we analyze the basic principles of the Bahá'í Faith, we will discover many similarities with, and a few differences from, Tolstoy's thinking which we have examined previously. A brief study of the Bahá'í teachings will help in understanding

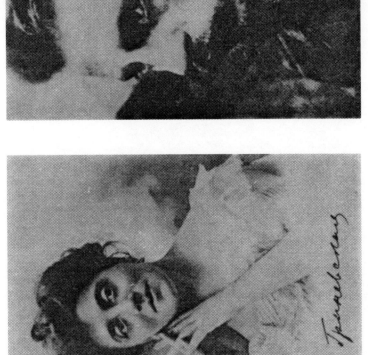

5. Rainer Maria Rilke, German poet, visited Tolstoy and sent him a pamphlet about the Bábís

4. The Russian poetess, Isabella Grinevskaya, author of the play The Báb, a copy of which she sent to Tolstoy

6. 'Azízu'lláh Jadhdháb, a Persian Bahá'í who visited Tolstoy in 1902 at Yasnaya Polyana, of which he gives a very interesting account

7. *Among Tolstoy's numerous visitors, the Russian writer A. Chekhov, at Gaspra (Crimea), 1901*

8. *Tolstoy at the table in his house at Yasnaya Polyana, 1907*

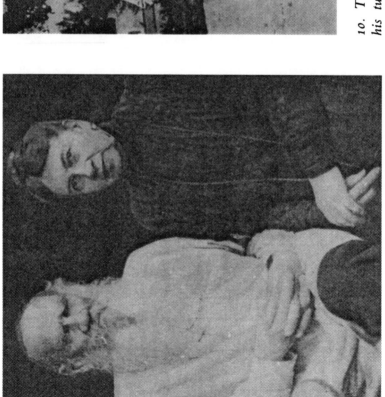

10. *Tolstoy with his secretary, Biryukov, and his two daughters, Ola and Leva; in the background, Tolstoy's own daughter, Alexandra*

9. *Tolstoy with his wife, Sophia Andreyevna*

the author's attitudes towards this religious movement. To this end, I have included as an Appendix a statement written in 1947 by Shoghi Effendi, Guardian of the Bahá'í Faith. It should be borne in mind that this statement gives a much more comprehensive account of the Bahá'í Faith than was generally available even to Bahá'ís of Tolstoy's time. Nonetheless, the basic principles were known.

We can see that many of Tolstoy's ideas were in harmony with the principles of this religious movement (among others: the need for a universal religion, independent investigation of the truth, harmony of religion and reason, the absence of clergy and ritual, universal peace). We have already seen that, in his letter to Mírzá Ríḍá Khán, Tolstoy proposes the acceptance by all humanity of one universal religion stripped of all rituals and forms of worship.

About three years earlier, he had written a letter to the French clergyman, Charles Bonet Maury, who had invited him to take part in the Congress of Religions which was to take place in Paris in 1900. In his reply, Tolstoy maintained the point of view that, in order to attain one single religion, such congresses were not only superfluous, but even harmful, and affirmed that the only way of getting there was for all men to seek out the truth individually:

The idea of the Congress is to unite the religions by external means – [he says in his letter, dated 23 November 1896] – while according to the idea of Religion, that is, the one universal Religion, unification can only take place from within; that is to say that debates and talks by various representatives of different religions cannot in any way help in uniting men in their relationship with God (rather, they produce the opposite effect), and the only way this union can be achieved is by sincere study by every individual of his relationship with the world, the Infinite, God . . . [4]

One single religion and the search for truth, which are basic teachings of the Bahá'í Faith, are also, as we have just seen, essential ideas in Tolstoy's philosophy.

On 27 May 1902 Tolstoy was in Gaspra, in the Crimea, where he was convalescing after a serious illness. That day he wrote in his *Diary*: 'Today a Persian pedlar called, a highly-cultivated man. He said he was a Bábí.'[5] This 'Persian pedlar', was a certain Kasím Bairamov. Unfortunately, there are no other details concerning this meeting; however, it is an important event, for it is the first time, to our knowledge, that a Bahá'í established personal contact with Tolstoy.

A few months later he received another visit, that of a Persian merchant by the name of Mírzá 'Azízu'lláh Jadhdháb Khurásání. In Tolstoy's *Diary* we find no reference to this encounter. On the other hand, the visitor has left a full account, including fascinating and amusing details. This account is written in Persian, and there has been no published translation of the text until now. In an archaic style redolent with flowery and courteous expressions, Jadhdháb describes his meeting with the author, gives an account of the exchange of views that took place between them, and the positive impression obtained from it:

On Sunday, 1st Ramadan 1320, being equivalent to 14 September 1902; cost of ticket to Tula: 11 roubles and 60 kopecks; cost of the carriage: 7 roubles and 60 kopecks; tip: 2 roubles.

On Monday, I set off again. On the way, lunch and supper: 2 roubles and 60 kopecks. Tuesday, the 16th, from Kurjk to Zayska, near Yasnaya Polyana. Wednesday evening, stop-over. Thursday morning, I set off in the direction of Yasnaya Polyana which is Count Leo Tolstoy's estate. (Expenses: 1 rouble.) In the train, the 'Konduktory' (railway company officials) told me: 'You will not be permitted to enter Yasnaya Polyana, as it's strictly forbidden by the government, even for his pupils, to visit Tolstoy. The train is not allowed to stop at the station for longer than a minute. Nobody is allowed to get off.' I said very humbly: 'I am an Iranian Bahá'í, and I need to visit him to deal with certain spiritual matters. I have come from 'Akká expressly for that purpose.'

The two 'Konduktory' in question were his pupils and friends. They thought and consulted with each other, and said to me, 'There's no other solution than to let you off at the signal-box, and we'll send one or two people to fetch you once the train has left the station.' I accepted and thanked them. When I got off at the signal-box, the night was cold and dark; it was raining and snowing. It was so cold that I was shivering in spite of my fur-coat, and it was so dark that if someone had made off with my suitcases, which were next to me, I wouldn't have seen him. After half-an-hour, or slightly more, two people came and in a friendly manner took my suitcases and we went together to the station. The station mechanic, who was a friend of the Count and who had sent these two men, lit a fire; the room warmed up, and we dried our clothes. In the morning, after having tea, and committing myself to God's care, I left my belongings at the station, and set off in a droshky towards Count Leo's dwelling in Yasnaya Polyana. On my way, I encountered some of his pupils who were returning, some in a droshky, others on foot, and they said to me: 'Don't go there. The police will not let you through.' But I carried on and arrived there. I got off the droshky by the front door of the house and greeted the policeman in Russian. He asked me why I had come, and I replied: 'I am an Iranian Bahá'í. I have to discuss certain spiritual and mystical matters with the Count.' He answered that he was not allowed to let anyone in. So I humbly requested him to ask someone to come so that I could transmit my message. This he accepted. A few minutes later a man came. After greeting me, I gathered it was Chertkov, the philosopher, who had been exiled from Russia for two years and who had just arrived to pay Count Tolstoy a visit. After a few questions and answers, and once he was informed that I had come from 'Akká, from 'Abdu'l-Bahá, and that I wished to transmit a message from him, he went back into the house. He came back after consulting the Count and said to the policeman on the Count's behalf: 'This person has come from 'Akká and has covered a great distance. He has not seen me before and is not one of my pupils, nor is he a Christian. He is a Bahá'í, and has come to talk about spiritual matters. Let him come in to converse with us, and then he will leave.' The policeman agreed, and Chertkov led me to a room which was

reserved for visitors. He confided to me that the Count had said to
him that, since I had had a difficult journey, it would be better if I
rested till midday, and we could have a conversation later at lunch-
time. I replied: 'I have never studied Russian, but I can speak it,
thanks to my journeys beyond the Caspian Sea, and I can read it a
little.' So I requested that he bring me the book Tolstoy had written
quite recently in which he rebelled against the Christian religious
authorities and which was the cause of all his problems, so that I could
study it meanwhile. He left and came back with the book. After I had
washed my hands and face, I was offered tea which I politely refused,
saying that I had already had some. I rested a while, and from nine
o'clock till midday I sat down to study the book and despite my
inadequate knowledge I understood the following: the Count
wondered if there was any objection in thinking like Jews and
Muslims, that Christ was like other prophets; he also added that the
people should not be made to believe in the story of the dove and
other superstitions for which the followers of other religions
reproach the Christians. This stance had provoked his excommunication by the religious authorities and his being kept under surveil-
lance. At one o'clock I was informed that he wished to see me. By a
curious coincidence it was the same day that his secretary had been
taken to Tula and imprisoned in order to prevent him from serving
the Count. Tolstoy's younger daughter had been sent there to try and
obtain his release. We made towards a house which was raised up to a
height of 3 aršines [1 aršine = about 71 centimetres]. Tolstoy was
sitting on a chair. It was a special chair, as he had his legs stretched out
because they gave him pain. After I arrived and we had greeted each
other, a separate table was prepared for Chertkov and myself. The
table was set according to their tradition. I said that not only did I not
drink alcohol but that for the last three years I had given up eating
meat. Smiling, the Count replied: 'I don't eat meat either. As for your
not eating meat, is that one of your new principles?' I replied: 'We
don't consider anything to be impure or forbidden, but 'Abdu'l-
Bahá wrote in a Tablet on that subject that man has not always been a
meat-eater.' I continued: 'God has not given man teeth and claws for
eating meat. There are many Hindus and Buddhists who do not eat
meat, and whose breath is better and more wholesome that others'. It
is not suitable that during man's short life in this world he should turn

his stomach into a cemetery for animals.' He ordered eggs to be prepared for us and during lunch he began to speak. First of all he said: 'I do not trust newspapers; some praise, others criticize. I wished to become informed of the Bábí and Bahá'í teachings on three occasions, and I wanted to write the truth according to the books I had received on that subject. The last time was about twelve days ago when I had the same discussion with Chertkov.' I replied that on three occasions I had undertaken journeys on 'Abdu'l-Bahá's instructions. The first time, the sacred teachings concerning universal peace were destined for the Prime Minister, Kuropatkin, and on that occasion, I learnt that it was forbidden either to see you or visit him. The second time, I wanted to see General Khamarov, but I had to abandon the idea; and this time, now that I am in your presence, it is precisely the twelfth day since I left 'Akká. He began to ask me questions: 'How do you consider the Báb? When did he appear? What were his claims?' I answered that the Báb was a young man, that his name was Siyyid 'Alí-Muḥammad, etc. . . [6]

He then asked what was the situation of Bahá'u'lláh's Faith following his death. I replied that it was advancing daily. He questioned me concerning Bahá'u'lláh's claims. I replied that Bahá'u'lláh was he who conversed on Sinai with the eternal Father and the Spirit of God. I continued: 'He is the heavenly father whom the children of Israel and the Christians are expecting; according to Shí'ih Muslims, he is the return or appearance of Ḥusayn; according to the Sunnís, the Báb is the manifestation of the Mahdí, and Bahá'u'lláh is the return of the Messiah; according to the Zoroastrians, he is the manifestation of Sháh Bahrám.'

In short, he is the one foretold by Isaiah and Daniel – Isaiah said that in this day, all nations will unite and will say to each other: 'Let us go to Carmel, the God of Israel has appeared; it is clear that he has come to save all the nations of the earth.' He questioned me about the new laws. I replied that the Holy Book of Bahá'u'lláh [the *Kitáb-i-Aqdás*] contains the new laws . . . The secondary laws are left to the Universal Assembly which is called the House of Justice. Among the laws are: unity of mankind, unity of religions, unity of language and systems of writing, unity of the races, equality of rights for men and women, abolition of national, religious, social, political and economic prejudices, etc. The education of boys and girls is obligatory. Among the laws, there is also that of choosing in each town, from among the members of the Bahá'í community, nine people responsible for administrative tasks, such as the education of children, improvement in the situation of the poor, etc.

He questioned me about acceptance of the Faith by non-Islámic nations. I replied: 'Among Jews many have accepted the Bahá'í Faith, in Hamadan, Yazd, Tehran, Khurásán (in Iran), likewise in the Caucasus and in America. I myself am a Jew from Khurásán. Among the Zoroastrians many have become Bahá'ís, both in Iran and in Bombay. Among the Christians, there are some in America, Paris, Germany and London, as well as Egypt.

'In 'Ishqábád, in Turkistán, on the Iranian border, there is a Bahá'í school. Pupils from all levels of society and of all religions are accepted, and the Bahá'ís cover the expenses of all the others.'

He questioned me concerning the station of 'Abdu'l-Bahá. I replied that he was the Interpreter of the sacred writings and the perfect example of a servant of Bahá'u'lláh, and that despite the clear Covenant of Bahá'u'lláh concerning 'Abdu'l-Bahá's rank, his brothers contested his authority. Tolstoy said it was normal that certain members even of Bahá'u'lláh's family should oppose him; and he continued: 'I myself have undertaken the education of a number of people, and my son in Petersburg strives day and night to obtain my condemnation and execution.'

Here now are the questions I asked him.

First of all, I transmitted to him 'Abdu'l-Bahá's message: 'Act that your name may leave a good memory in the world of religion. Many philosophers have come, each one raising a flag, let us say five metres high. You have raised a flag ten metres high; immerse yourself in the ocean of unity, so that you may remain confirmed eternally.'

My second question was: 'In the light of the information I have just given you, what is your opinion concerning Bahá'u'lláh?'

He raised his hands and replied: 'How could I deny him? I have wished to educate certain Russians, and I have been subjected to house-arrest, with police installed in order to ensure no one visits me. Obviously this cause will conquer the whole world. I myself have already accepted Muhammad.'

Then he added: 'Send me more writings.'

I replied: 'I have not studied Russian and the other European languages, but Mírzá 'Alí-Akhbar Nakhjavání lives in Bákú. I will give him your address, so that he can translate the holy writings and send them on to you.' He replied: 'I asked Chertkov these questions a few days ago; so your arrival has been like telepathy between our two hearts. For my part, give my greetings and respect to the "velikij Uchitel" (Great Master) 'Abdu'l-Bahá. I will write about this new religion in my books.' After that, he gave me some of his photographs as well as a few books. Then I had a brief conversation with his doctor, with his secretary who had just been released that same afternoon, and also with the Count's youngest daughter. I had another short conversation with Chertkov, concerning my travels in India and the harshness and difficulties of Bahá'u'lláh's imprisonment.

Towards sunset, I took my leave. Ticket from Zayska to Bákú: 14 roubles and 70 kopecks. Cost of the droshky: 1 rouble and 75 kopecks. Date: 19 September 1902.[7]

By means of this account, which is interesting from many points of view, we realize that Tolstoy was known and admired by a number of Bahá'ís. Some of his ideas being in agreement with Bahá'í principles, several believers on an individual basis tried to establish contact with him, in order to express their esteem and to convey to him the universality of Bahá'u'lláh's message.

4

Awareness or Criticism?

During the years 1903–1906, Tolstoy fluctuated in his relationship with this new religious movement. The discovery of certain texts which contained principles which were not in accord with his ideas had perhaps momentarily disenchanted the author. Information about the Bahá'í Faith continued to reach him, not only from Persia, but also from Europe. In Russia itself, the poetess Isabella Arkadevna Grinevskaya, author of numerous dramas and tragedies and an ardent admirer of Tolstoy, sent him in 1903 a dramatic poem which she had just composed, entitled *The Báb*. In the succeeding years this drama was produced with great success in the literary and artistic theatre of St Petersburg, and in Russia's principal theatres. The impact of this play was such that it continued to be acted even after the Russian Revolution.

In his reply to the poetess, Tolstoy expressed his opinion both of the theatrical work and of the Báb's teachings. In his correspondence of 22 October 1903, one reads:

Very happy that V. V. Stasov has conveyed to you the fine impression your book made on me, and I thank you for sending it to me. I have known of the Bábís for a long time, and am much interested in their teachings. It seems to me that these teachings, like all rationalist, social and religious teachings that have arisen recently out of the old religions which have been distorted by the priests, such as Brahmanism, Buddhism, Judaism, Christianity and Islám, have a great future, above all because they have rejected all these monstrous hierarchies which divide the old religions, and they aspire to come together into one single religion common to the whole of mankind. That is why the Bábí teachings, insofar as they reject the old Muslim superstitions and do not establish any new ones (unfortunately something similar may be perceived in the presentation of the Báb's teachings), and insofar as they hold fast to their main and fundamental ideas of brotherhood, equality and love, are assured a great future. In Islám there has recently been an intense spiritual renewal. I know that one such movement exists in French Africa and that it has a name (which I have forgotten) and its own prophet.

There's another movement in India, in Lahore. It also has its prophet and publishes its own paper, *Review of Religions*. Both these religious doctrines contain nothing new, and at the same time, they do not set themselves as their main aim to change the concept of the world, nor, consequently, to transform social relationships – by contrast, what I perceive in Bábísm is quite different, not so much in the theory of its teachings but in its practice, as far as I know it. And for this reason, I sympathize with all my heart with Bábísm, insofar as it preaches brotherhood and equality between all men, and the sacrifice of material life in the service of God.[1]

The following year Tolstoy continued to pursue his research on the teachings of the Founder of the Bahá'í Faith. In a letter addressed to a Muslim dignitary, the Indian Mufti Muḥammad Sadíq, editor of the paper, *Review of Religions*, he writes as follows: 'Dear Sir, thank you for the *Review of Religions*. I am very interested in your work. Do you know the teachings of Bahá'u'lláh, and what do you think of them?'[2] The exchange of information does not seem to have been pursued, as Tolstoy's correspondence nowhere mentions his having received a reply from this religious dignitary.

On 4 April 1904 a French lawyer, Hippolyte Dreyfus, sent Tolstoy his translation of Bahá'u'lláh's *Kitáb-i-Íqán*, entitled *Le*

Livre de la Certitude. Reading this book produced a bad impression on Tolstoy, and worked in him a negative reaction which he expressed in these terms, in his reply dated 18 April 1904:

Sir,

Thank you for sending me the book by Bahá'u'lláh. I regret that I am obliged to say that reading this book has completely put me off Bahá'u'lláh's teachings. This book merely contains insignificant and pretentious phrases which have no other purpose but to confirm the old superstitions which are completely devoid of any moral and religious content, in the true sense of that word. Nevertheless, I am very grateful for your letter and the book and please accept my warmest regards.[3]

On analyzing the book in question, one can better comprehend Tolstoy's surprising reaction. It is a long letter written by Bahá'u'lláh to one of the Báb's uncles who had not yet accepted his nephew's message, and who had asked Bahá'u'lláh for proofs concerning the claims of His Forerunner. In this letter Bahá'u'lláh demonstrates that the station of the Báb is the same as that of the other Prophets of the past.

He thus reaffirms the divinity of Christ, not as the second person of the Trinity, but as God's Messenger (and thus not a man like others); and similarly that of all the divine Messengers: Abraham, Moses, Muḥammad, etc. He explains certain passages from the Old and New Testaments, from the Qur'án and the Ḥadíth (Muslim Traditions), and he shows how all the Prophets can be considered as one and the same entity, insofar as they are all representatives, to a complementary degree, of the Divine Spirit which animates them.

In addition, since the book was addressed to a S͟hí'ih Muslim, it was adapted to this person's mentality and upbringing. Tolstoy, therefore, could not understand all the allusions in this work, nor could he accept the idea that Christ and the other Founders of religion were superior in rank to other men, as he had so often repeated and affirmed in his works which deal with this subject.

Still under the shock of this discovery, Tolstoy replied in these terms to one of his friends, the American author Ernest Crosby, who had sent him 'an interesting book, a résumé by the present-day leader of the Bahá'ís 'Abbas Effendi,'[4] dated 31 July 1904: *'Dear friend, I was very interested by Bahá'ísm, and I know all about it. I believe this sect has no future . . .'*[5]

Despite the apparent indifference and self-satisfied attitude which is evident in these lines, Tolstoy did not cease to investigate the validity and implications of these teachings. In his letters we find him constantly preoccupied about the opinion his correspondents have on the subject, and anxious to obtain further information from them. Thus in a letter addressed to the Mufti of Cairo, Muḥammad 'Abduh, he writes among other things: 'What do you think about the teachings of the Báb and Bahá'u'lláh and their followers?'[6]

Dusan Petrovic Makovitsky was Tolstoy's doctor from 1904 to 1910. He was also a close friend and took constant care of him. Makovitsky has left a private diary in which he relates interesting incidents and conversations which Tolstoy often had with him and other members of his circle. There are also a few precious references to the relationship between the great author and the Bahá'í Faith. On 1 February 1905 the doctor notes in his *Journal*: 'at the house at tea-time, Leo Nicolaevich brought me a booklet in English, *Hidden Words*. "Here is something about Bábísm," he said. "They are pompous words. Look and you'll see what it's about."'[7] The booklet Tolstoy was referring to is a brief work revealed by Bahá'u'lláh.[8] However, the author included one of the Hidden Words in his compilation, *Reading Programme for Every Day*. On 14 June, under the title, 'Bábí Tablets', this quotation appears: 'Breathe not the sins of others so long as thou art thyself a sinner.'[9]

On another occasion, Makovitsky overheard a conversation between Tolstoy and Victor Lebrun, a young Frenchman who had enthusiastically adopted Tolstoy's ideas:

> Leo Nicolaevich: I've received a letter from Nabokov, a Russian in Chicago, concerning Bábísm . . . The son of the Founder of the Bahá'í Sect, who was executed in Persia, lives in 'Akká in Syria. He also sent me a little pamphlet in English, an outline of Bahá'ísm.
>
> Lebrun: Bahá'ísm, is that Islám purified?
>
> Leo Nicolaevich: Yes, rationalized. Nabokov writes to me that there is a certain resemblance between their teachings and my opinions.[10]

The son of the Founder of the Bahá'í Faith of whom Tolstoy speaks is 'Abdu'l-Bahá, but the writer is mistaken in saying that his father was executed in Persia; he certainly means to refer to the Báb. In any case, this indicates superficial knowledge on his part.

While occasionally evincing fluctuations and changes of opinion, Tolstoy once again started at this time to hold the Bahá'í Faith in great esteem. Indeed, from this time on, he considered it as a purifying reform of Islám, and in this connection, Makovitsky describes a conversation between Tolstoy and S.D. Nikolayev thus:[11]

> After lunch, Nikolayev showed Leo Nicolaevich a few passages from the proofs of Tolstoy's essay, 'On the Significance of the Russian Revolution.' In this article, Muhammad is compared with Christ and Buddha, and Islám with Christianity and Buddhism. The two words, Muhammad and Islám, have been crossed out, and then written in again. Nikolayev asked: 'What are we to think of that? What are we going to do about it?' Leo Nicolaevich: 'Concerning the word Islám, I'm not sure . . . I consider Islám as a form of Christianity, which has emerged from apocryphal Christian traditions: the struggle against the Trinity and iconoclasm. Whatever has passed into Islám from Christianity is good, whatever comes from

12. *Hippolyte Dreyfus, the first French Bahá'í, sent Tolstoy his book* Essai sur le Bahá'isme

11. *Youness Khan, 'Abdu'l-Bahá's secretary, who contributed to Tolstoy's knowledge of the Bahá'í teachings*

14. *Tolstoy leafing through the heavy mail which he daily received from all parts of the world*

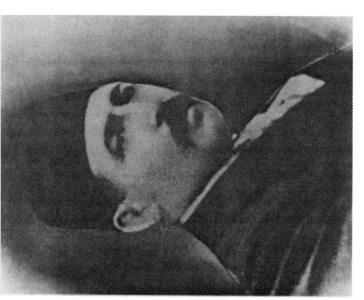

13. *'Alí-Akhbar Nakhjavání, who conducted a lengthy correspondence with Tolstoy during the last two years of the author's life*

Muḥammad is coarse. The doctrine of the Muslim sects of Bábísm
. . . is purely Christian.' Nikolayev suggested inserting the words 'in
part'. Leo Nicolaevich thought a while, agreed and added 'in part
Islám (Bábísm)'.[12]

Makovitsky refers to the treatise, 'On the Significance of the
Russian Revolution', written by Tolstoy in 1906. The
definitive version of this work confirms what the author's
doctor says. In the middle of the last chapter, devoted to the
reaffirmation of his beliefs, Tolstoy writes:

To consciously turn from the seduction of human power to
obedience to God's single and supreme power is to recognize the
need in one's self, always and everywhere, of God's eternal laws.
This need exists in the same way in all teachings: in Brahmanism,
Buddhism, Confucianism, Taoism, Christianity, in part in Islám
(Bábísm) . . . [13]

In another small treatise, unpublished and written in 1905
under the title 'The How and Why of Living', Tolstoy had
explained that wisdom can be found in the new religious
reforms, including Bábísm:

It (wisdom) can be found in the teachings of Rousseau, Kant,
Channing, in the teachings of the Neo-Buddhists, Neo-Brahmins,
Bábís and of thousands of people who understand and enlighten the
religious teachings of old.[14]

In the light of all the information Tolstoy had collected
about the Bahá'í Faith, it is surprising to observe that on the
envelope for a letter the author intended to send to Mrs.
Thornburgh-Cropper, an American Bahá'í living in England,
he had noted the following sentence: 'Reply thanking her for
her letter. Who is 'Abbás Effendi?'[15] We know that Tolstoy had
often heard mention of this person who is so important to the
history of the Bahá'í Faith. He had previously had the
testimonies of Ernest Crosby who had sent him some of
'Abbás Effendi's writings, and of Makovitsky who reproduces

in his diary a conversation between Tolstoy and his friends in which Tolstoy speaks of the son of the Founder of Bahá'ísm, living in 'Akká in Syria. Besides this, Tolstoy often contradicts himself during this period. First he assures Crosby that he knows all about the Bahá'í Faith. Then he forgets the name of its religious leader, saying that this sect has no future; a little later he writes that the Bahá'í Faith is Islám's message purified, its teachings purely Christian.

We must not forget that Tolstoy was a being in evolution. Only then can we justify his radical changes of opinion.

5

On the Threshold of Acceptance?

On 4 December 1908 Tolstoy received a letter from a young student of Persian origin living in Moscow. Fridul K͟hán Badalbekov (such was his name) had written to ask him three important questions of a spiritual nature: 1) How to understand God; 2) What awaits us after death; 3) What is the place of Islám among the great religions.

In his reply Tolstoy reaffirms his concept of God as Love, explains the reasons for his belief in life after death, maintains that Islám, like the other religions, has distorted the truth, and introduces his correspondent to the Bahá'í Faith which he defines as one of the highest and purest of religious teachings. The letter which follows marks perhaps a turning-point in Tolstoy's understanding and attitude towards the Bahá'í Faith:

In reply to the first question, how to understand the word 'God', I am sending you a little compilation of texts, selected by myself and based on my *Reading Programme*. In this book I have put together the thoughts concerning God with which I am in agreement. In my opinion one must above all free oneself from the idea of God conceived as a personal being, a concept which exists in both Christianity and Islám.

The concept of God which comes closest to my understanding and which answers best to the requirements of the mind and heart of man is that expressed in the First Epistle of John, namely, that 'God is Love'. Thus the more man is filled with love, the more God dwells within him and the more such a man can understand God. This thought is more or less expressed in all religions, including Islám.

Concerning your second question, what awaits us after death, I can only reply that, on dying, we return where we came from, that is to say, towards God. Now, this God to whom we return is love. That is why, when we die, we can expect nothing else but good.

To your third question, I reply that, in my opinion, Islám, like all religions, Brahmanism, Buddhism, Confucianism, etc., contains the great eternal truths; but like all other religions Islám has, by means of rituals and deceit, added to its teachings superstitions which are gross distortions of the truth. The excellent booklet entitled *The Sayings of Muḥammad*, edited by 'Abdu'lláh Al-Mamun Alsuhráh Wardy [Suhrawardy] and published in London, has greatly helped me form an idea of Islám.

Bábísm, which has evolved into Bahá'ísm (Bahá'u'lláh), and which has its roots in Islám, is one of the highest and purest of religious teachings. I will be very happy if you find my reply satisfying.[1]

The last sentence of the letter, 'Bahá'ísm . . . is one of the highest and purest of religious teachings', is of great interest. Indeed, in the letter from the young Persian student there was no reference to this religion, which was taboo in a country where it was subject to the worst persecutions. Yet Tolstoy not only mentions its existence but, moreover, greatly praises it. Rare were the instances when his pen would write such enthusiastic praise for a contemporary religious movement.

The analysis of the last two years of Tolstoy's life is of great interest for the understanding of his spiritual development.

At this point he had arrived at a stage where we can assume that he no longer considered himself a Christian. Until this time, while accepting the other religions as true, he felt himself closer to Christ's teachings. Earlier, when his correspondents used to ask his opinion about the true religion, Tolstoy would reply by advising them to read the Gospels carefully. As from 1909, he declares that he has no particular bias towards Christianity, and no longer attaches a great value to the Gospels. In this connection the letter he wrote that July to the Polish painter, Jan Styka, is particularly interesting. The text of this confession, which is at once so surprising and clear, is as follows:

Dear friend,

I received the reproductions of your beautiful picture. I admire its execution and thank you for the idea. Above all, I thank you for your kind feelings towards me.

I think the fact that you reproach me for basing my religious convictions on a book, the Gospels, stems from a misunderstanding. You ask me if I really think every enlightened man has no other path to self-perfection available than that outlined in the Gospels. I have never had such an idea. To me, Jesus' teachings are merely one of the beautiful and great religious teachings we have received from antiquity, be it Egyptian, Jewish, Hindu, Chinese or Greek. Jesus' two great principles: love of God, that is to say, of absolute perfection, and love of one's neighbour, that is to say, of all men without distinction (nor could it be otherwise, since these two principles form the basis of true religion and true morality) – these principles have been preached, in various ways, by all the sages of the world, by the ancients: Krishna, Buddha, Lao-Tse, Confucius, Socrates, Plato, Marcus Aurelius, Epictetus, and also similarly by modern thinkers (to name only a few): Rousseau, Pascal, Kant, Emerson, Channing and many, many others.

Religious and moral truth is everywhere and always the same, and I try to make it my own wherever I find it, without any preference for Christianity. If I have been particularly interested in Christ's teachings, it is because, first, I was born and have lived among Christians, and second, I have found a great mental pleasure in extricating, as far as I have been able, the true teachings from the surprising distortions which have been carried out by the churches on these unfortunate teachings. I very much regret that one of my books to which I am conceited enough to attach great importance has not been translated into French, and that I can only send it to you in Russian and German. From this book, entitled *For Every Day*, and consisting of thoughts and maxims concerning religion and morality from several hundred authors, both ancient and modern, among which are to be found only a few verses from the Gospels, you will be able to judge how far I am from attaching an exceptional value to the Gospels.[2]

In the light of this letter one can no longer assert, without risk of contradicting oneself, that Tolstoy remained a Christian to the end of his life. The only reason which could lead one to suppose an identification of the author with Christianity is, according to him, this mental pleasure which encouraged him to distinguish the truth from the false interpretations of the church in whose bosom he was born.

According to Makovitsky, Tolstoy even declares that he does not like the Gospels: 'Just as I passionately loved the Gospels, now decidedly, I do not like them anymore, because they are full of contradictions.'[3]

Romain Rolland writes in his book *La Vie de Tolstoï* that in the last two years of the author's life he became much closer to the other religions, and in particular, to the Bahá'í Faith; in the chapter entitled 'Asia's Reply to Leo Tolstoy', the author quotes certain extracts from letters, proving that Tolstoy had a real interest in the Bahá'í Faith.

In 1909 Tolstoy read much about the Bahá'í Faith. On 24 January he noted in his *Diary*: 'Now I have just read *Fellowship*. Many good things. Bahá'í very interesting.'[4]

In the space of one year, between March 1909 and February 1910, there exist to our knowledge no fewer than sixteen letters written by the Count in which there are references to and evaluations of the Bahá'í Faith, which show that the Bahá'í Faith occupied at that time an important place in Tolstoy's thinking.

On 16 March 1909 he wrote to Mrs E.E. Velikova whose two sons had asked her permission to convert to Islám. In this letter, after repeating that all religions are true in their essence, Tolstoy informs the lady that there exist in Islám two very interesting movements:

I do not know if you and your children are acquainted with two doctrines within Islám of which I have knowledge and which aspire to the same goal: to free the highest and most fundamental truths from the errors and superstitions which obscure them. These two movements have undergone and are for this reason undergoing persecution. One of these two doctrines is that of the Bábís. Bábísm, which originated in Persia, has spread in Turkey where it has also suffered persecution, and it is now represented by Bahá'u'lláh's son who lives in 'Akká. This doctrine recognizes no external way of worshipping God; it considers that all men are brothers, and recognizes one single religion of love, common to all humanity.[5]

On the same day, Tolstoy once again spread knowledge of the Bahá'í teachings, in a letter addressed to the Tartar writer M. J. Krymbayev, who was of the opinion that Islám was going in the opposite direction to science, and that it was in the process of destroying itself: after speaking of the distortion of the Muslim teachings, Tolstoy continues:

There exists the Bábí sect whose religious teachings are of a very high order. The successor to the Báb's cause, Bahá'u'lláh, was exiled by the Turkish authorities to 'Akká where his son now lives. The members of this sect recognize no external form of religion, and the basis of religion is, according to them, the goodness of life, that is to say, love for one's neighbour, and non-participation in the evil projects carried out by governments . . .*[6]

In this letter, Tolstoy speaks of the Bahá'í Faith as a sect of Islám. It was normal that, barely fifty years after its founding, people from the West considered it as a Muslim sect. In Tolstoy's terminology, the word 'sect' has no pejorative

* see below, pp. 46–7, 63–4 for the Bahá'í principle of obedience to government.

meaning; on the contrary, in the last two letters the writer speaks very highly of the Bahá'í Faith.

On 14 May 1909 Tolstoy sent two books, *The Gospel of Rama-Krishna* by Swami Abhedäanda, and *Essai sur le Bahá'ísme* (Essay on Bahá'ísm) by Hippolyte Dreyfus, to his close friend, J. J. Gorbunov-Posadov, accompanied by the following letter:

Dear Ivan Ivanovich,

I am sending you the book about Krishna. Decide for yourself what needs cutting. All the same, it will be a useful book. I am also sending you a book in French about the Bahá'ís. The book as a whole is bad, but one can use certain things for the one translated from the English. You must absolutely include in it the admirable chapter on pages 79–80.[7]

The chapter in the essay by Dreyfus to which Tolstoy refers and which he seems to appreciate so highly is devoted to the analysis of patriotism as a social phenomenon, and to the Bahá'í viewpoint regarding patriotic sentiment. Tolstoy's point of view is in this field very close to the Bahá'í principles. That is why the author insisted that Gorbunov should include it in the work he intended to publish. Tolstoy had written two little treatises on the same subject, the first entitled *Patriotism or Peace?*, and the second *Patriotism and Government*. A look at these texts will enable us to discover the similarities and differences between the two concepts.

Hippolyte Dreyfus introduces his brief outline thus:

We said earlier that the two pillars on which Bahá'í sociology rests are love and work. We have likewise seen how this love is manifested first in the relationships which the Bahá'í must maintain with different peoples, to whatever race or sect they may belong, and this quite naturally leads us to examine the place which the idea of one's country occupies in Bahá'u'lláh's teachings.

Dreyfus continues his essay, and reaffirms the Bahá'í point of view concerning patriotism:

Until now, few ideas have been so productive of noble deeds, of sublime devotion, but few also, I fear, are responsible for so much blind fanaticism and fratricidal struggles. It happens, alas, all too frequently that the noble ideas of the masses become in the hands of unscrupulous individualists or minorities with vested interests too easy an instrument for the satisfaction of their personal ambitions. Thus, one finds in the Ishráqát ('Splendours'), a Tablet of Bahá'u'lláh: 'The most glorious fruit of the tree of knowledge is this exalted word: Of one tree are all ye the fruit, and of one bough the leaves. Let not man glory in this that he loveth his country, let him rather glory in this that he loveth his kind.' What does this mean, if not that this love of one's country which lies instinctively in the heart of each individual, this imperative need to defend the land of one's birth against the dangers which threaten it, and which is, in the final analysis, but a form of the instinct for self-preservation, is insufficient. Any man worthy of the name must go further: he must prove capable of feeling a similar love for the whole world. Will it be necessary, as some claim, to treat such a person as perverted, and are there not barriers between internationalism and antipatriotism? To love one's village as much as one's home, one's country as much as one's village, and the whole world as much as one's country, does not mean that one does not love one's home. But this love of one's home, so natural that one may say it is common both to men and animals, should give birth, along with respect for one's neighbour's home, to an equally sincere love of one's country. Ready to welcome all our brothers in our home, we must equally divest ourselves of the prejudices which make us feel strangers in their homes, and we must manage to think of the whole world as our common fatherland, which the difficulty of the means of communication and the yet precarious nature of our individual civilizations have subjected to temporary and artificial divisions. Thus, the love of one's country will lose its violent and hostile character, and it will merely tend to develop the potentialities of each nation, as an integral part of the great universal country.[8]

Tolstoy begins his treatise *Patriotism or Peace?* by maintaining the idea that patriotism brings war, and that peace will not reign on earth as long as people remain attached to their own country above all else. He compares men to children whom one asks to choose between two things which attract them. The children reply naively that they want both. Thus, if one asks adults which they prefer, patriotism or peace, they reply: patriotism and peace. So men do not understand that love for a particular country is not a factor for peace, because at the first occasion for disagreement with another country, they will feel obliged to take sides on behalf of their own. Patriotism is, basically, a form of selfishness. Men often maintain that patriotism has enabled people to unite. To this Tolstoy replies by maintaining the opposite theory: patriotism divides instead of uniting, for without patriotism, there would be no nationalism which is the primary cause of war. Men, insists the author, have forgotten the teachings of the great divine messengers who have always, without exception, taught universal love.

In the treatise *Patriotism and Government* Tolstoy recalls that patriotism was undoubtedly commendable when weak nations united to get rid of the invader, but the law of brotherhood and love was promulgated two thousand years ago, and so it is now time to abandon national prejudices. Governments have a vested interest in preserving and encouraging all forms of patriotism, because it is part of their *raison d'être*. Men would be happier, if they were not dependent on a power which obliges them to kill their fellow-men, in order to take possession of other peoples' property.

Although in this field Tolstoy's ideas seem to come close to Bahá'í principles, one can observe that there is a considerable difference between the two concepts. Concerning two points, Tolstoy is in agreement with the Bahá'í teachings: in the rejection of an exclusive love for one particular country, and in the need to serve humanity without distinction of race or nationality. But Tolstoy's anarchic pacifism does not agree with Bahá'u'lláh's teachings which encourage believers to respect the authority of their respective governments on whom they depend, while working both for the realization of the unity of mankind and of the universal peace announced by Bahá'u'lláh in His writings.

The idea of a universal religion adopted by all peoples is one of the arguments with which Tolstoy deals most in his correspondence during this period. For example, he mentions it in a letter written to a member of the French Parliament, Philippe Grenier, who had confided in him his intention to convert to Islám, and to work for the unity of men in one single religion. In his reply, dated 24 March 1909, Tolstoy informs Grenier that there already exists a religious movement which has this same aim:

> The idea you express – namely that there are no different religions, but that there is only one single religion – is an idea which is becoming more and more widespread, especially among the Muslims.
>
> There are those who continue the Báb's teachings – Bahá'u'lláh who is in exile in 'Akká and the Muslims of Kazan, in Russia, who call themselves God's Regiment, whose principal tenet is the universality of religions . . . [9]

Two months later, Tolstoy received a letter from P.P. Kartushin, a friend of Cossack origin, enclosing an excerpt from a work by Bahá'u'lláh. This was the *Kitáb-i-Aqdás* (The Most Holy Book), as one may guess from a note at the bottom of the page, which appears in his correspondence. The perusal of this text irritated Tolstoy, and in his reply to Kartushin, he expressed his disappointment thus:

> I have found this same defect which one encounters with the Theosophists, Spiritualists and Mystics, to some extent in Koles-

nicenko's letter and to the greatest, quite repugnant and provoking extent, in the following extract from Laukh:

'Love one another and do to others that which you desire for yourself.' I understand [writes Tolstoy] that these exalted words constitute a great step forward in a religious movement, but to assert that God, according to Bahá'u'lláh's very own terms, 'is an inaccessible mystery which none will ever understand', is a useless complication of a truth which everyone should understand: be they young, old, educated or illiterate people. The knowledge of God is the most precious thing in the world . . . [10]

The *Kitáb-i-Aqdás* (which Tolstoy incorrectly calls the book of Laukh, believing it to concern a person called Laukh, whereas in Persian the word means 'Tablet' or 'Epistle') is the Book of Laws decreed by Bahá'u'lláh. These laws are destined for a united world, and are intended to govern the principal activities of men in a future society. Tolstoy, the anarchist, rebels against these precepts set forth by a man who calls himself a Messenger of God. According to him, the application of the commandment 'Love your neighbour as yourself' is sufficient. There is no need for either social institutions or specific laws. Furthermore, Tolstoy does not conceive of God as an inaccessible and unknowable being; God is to be found in man's heart, and an intermediary between man and God is in no way necessary. Bahá'u'lláh says in His Writings that men, being veiled by their physical limitations, are unable to 'see God with their own eyes, or hear His melody with their own ears'.[11] Thus this inaccessible Essence periodically sends messengers who remind men of the eternal truths and give laws adapted to the level of development of humanity.

In spite of these divergences in their ideas, Tolstoy wrote to Artpet, an author and editor of books dealing with the Orient, and asked him for a book entitled *The Bábí Sect*,[12] along with some other titles.

It seems that there was no direct correspondence between Tolstoy and 'Abdu'l-Bahá. There do exist, however, a few Tablets of 'Abdu'l-Bahá, addressed to Bahá'í believers, in which there is mention of Tolstoy.

A Bahá'í of Persian origin, Mírzá 'Alí-Akhbar Nakhjavání, who had intended to get into contact with Tolstoy, wrote to 'Abdu'l-Bahá for advice. In his answer, 'Abdu'l-Bahá encouraged this believer to begin the correspondence:

Always extend to Count Tolstoy loving and heartfelt greetings, and treat him with the utmost courtesy, as we are indeed commanded to behave in this way. Perchance he may become fairminded. There are signs that his attitude hath improved and moderated. It is hoped that, God willing, it may improve further and that he may speak with justice about this Cause. It might be beneficial if thou wert to despatch to him, and others like him, the letter of this servant addressed to the believers of the East and the West, which is translated and published in Russian.[13]

Nakhjavání therefore sent Tolstoy 'Abdu'l-Bahá's Tablet, 'Call to the Bahá'ís of the East and West'.[14] Tolstoy replied, declaring that he was very interested in the Bahá'í teachings, and that he intended to write a book about the Báb and the Bahá'í Faith. The following letter addressed to 'Mamed-khanov'[15] is dated 22 September 1909:

I have received your letter and at the same time, the book by 'Abdu'l-Bahá, 'Abbás Effendi: 'Call to the Bahá'ís of the East and West'. If what you are writing is not about something else, then I shall be most happy to receive it, because I am very interested in the teachings of Bahá'ísm. What the venerable 'Abdu'l-Bahá expressed in his sermon in 'Akká, namely that I gave land to the peasants is, unfortunately, not so, since, having children who were counting on inheriting my possessions upon my death, and considering that I had no right to do that, in 1881 I gave my heirs leave to dispose of my property as if I were dead. In this way, I freed myself of all property ownership.

Most happy to be in touch with you, since recently I have been concerned with the publishing of a book about the Báb and Bahá'ísm.[16]

It is not known what the book was that Tolstoy was in the process of writing about the Báb and the Bahá'í Faith, and it may be that the author only intended to write it. Probably, for lack of time, he was unable to complete the work.

Around the middle of the month of October, Tolstoy received another book from Artpet, entitled *Imámate: Land of the Imám Worshippers*, and edited in Alexandropol during that same year; it is perhaps to this book that he refers, again in his *Diary*, on 18 October 1909: 'I have received an interesting book about the Báb and Bahá'u'lláh. I haven't finished it yet.'[17]

On the previous day, Makovitsky noted in his diary that Tolstoy had spoken of this book among his attendants:

Leo Nicolaevich spoke of a book in Russian about Bahá'ísm which he had just received from Bákú, and he shook his head. Alexandra Lvovna asked him why he had shaken his head, and Leo Nicolaevich answered: 'Bahá'ísm is a lofty message, written in an emphatic Oriental style, stating that there must not be any violence (it appears therein that evil cannot be vanquished by violence). The main adversaries of religion are not those who kill, but those who alter religion, the teachings, as here (in Bahá'ísm) the sons' dispute. Bahá'u'lláh had two sons (two dead), and they argue who among them is the true heir of the father's teachings, and they slander each other. The same thing happened here with Jesus Christ, and with Paul. The questions asked by Christ were eternal, whereas Paul's interests were petty.'[18]

Artpet's book, whose sources are unknown to us, therefore serves as the basis of this surprising interpretation by Tolstoy of the events which took place after Bahá'u'lláh's death. What is certain is that in the Tablet of the Branch[19] Bahá'u'lláh had referred to 'Abdu'l-Bahá as his successor and unique interpreter.

As for 'Abdu'l-Bahá's attitude, we know from several

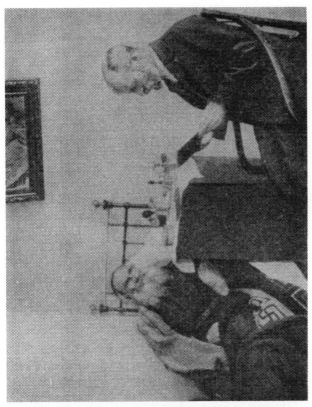

16. *Makovitsky reading to Tolstoy*

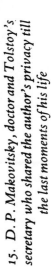

15. *D. P. Makovitsky, doctor and Tolstoy's secretary who shared the author's privacy till the last moments of his life*

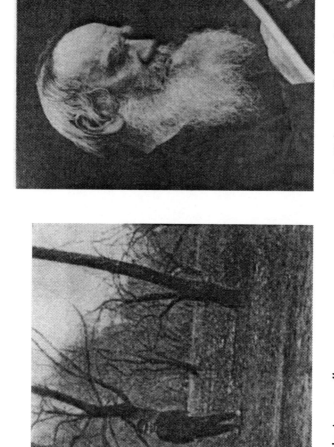

18. *Tolstoy reading, the last year of his life*

17. *At leisure, playing gorodky, 1909*

sources, including the diary of Youness Khan, his secretary, that for a long time he kept hidden from the believers the plots and the suffering which his half-brother made him undergo, and that as long as he had to deal with him, he always treated his half-brother with great generosity and kindness.

In any event, the rebellion of 'Abdu'l-Bahá's half-brother left no trace in the history of the Bahá'í movement, nor does it seem to have affected Tolstoy for very long, since a few days later he continued his correspondence with Nakhjavání. The Bahá'í sent him from Bákú his translations of a few Tablets of Bahá'u'lláh and 'Abdu'l-Bahá, and among Tolstoy's letters we find his reply written in the third person, though the handwriting is that of Tolstoy: 'L(eo) N(icolaevich) thanks you for sending the highly interesting book and manuscript, and sends you a few works of which he is the author.'[20]

On 12 October 1909 Tolstoy wrote to his friend F.A. Zheltov, to whom he explained that, unfortunately, all religions had been distorted but that there existed purifying movements, and 'above all, the pure and devoted teachings of the Báb's pupil – Bahá'u'lláh'.[21]

A month later Nakhjavání sent another translation of a Tablet by Bahá'u'lláh.[22] Once again, the author reacted negatively to a writing which contains counsels and exhortations with regard to human conduct; here is Tolstoy's reply:

I very much regret not being able to set a great value on the ideas you sent me. There's absolutely no sense in it. Generally, the more I become acquainted with the Bahá'í teachings the less I appreciate them, and that is why I hesitate to write a book on this subject.[23]

However, two months after this, in a letter addressed to the same correspondent, we find that Tolstoy's attitude has changed once again. In fact, he reaffirms his plan to write a book about the Bahá'í teachings:

Thank you very much for your letter and the book (I haven't yet received the book). I am putting together a series of approachable little books, from the point of view of both price and contents, dealing with the most important religious doctrines in the world. I wish to compose a book about the Bahá'ís, which is why I am glad to have received documentation indispensable to this publication.[24]

One must also note that at this late period in Tolstoy's life the three central figures of this new religious revelation had acquired their true importance in his mind, after so often confusing their functions and their rôles.

Once again, Makovitsky's precious testimony helps us. The scene took place on 24 November 1909:

After the meal Olga Konstantinova asked who was Bahá'u'lláh. Leo Nicolaevich answered: 'The Báb was the Forerunner (John the Baptist), and the true master was Bahá'u'lláh. The present leader of the Bábís is the son of Bahá'u'lláh, 'Abbás Effendi. Bahá'u'lláh was greater.'[25]

Here is a clear picture of the principal figures of the Bahá'í Faith. One need only add that, in His writings, Bahá'u'lláh considered the Báb not only as His forerunner, but also as a Messenger of God, holding the same rank as the other founders of religion.

In the last year of his life, Tolstoy seems to have abandoned the negative attitude towards the Bahá'í Faith which he had occasionally evinced in the past. Henceforth he had many writings on the subject at his disposal, and he was therefore able to have a more or less precise idea of Bahá'í aims and principles. Thus, in a letter dated 5 January 1910 and addressed to Muḥammad Fatikh Murtazín, a Mullá from Sámarrá, Tolstoy does not hesitate to quote Bahá'u'lláh's name alongside those of Buddha, Jesus, Confucius and Muḥammad:

I shall try, as far as I am able, to reply to your five questions.

First question: I think the Muslims are quite right not to acknow-
ledge God in three persons.

Second question: All men have been sent by God to carry out his
purpose. Thus both the simplest men and the wisest and most saintly
are sent by God. Muḥammad in Arabia, Jesus in Judea, Buddha in
India, Confucius in China, Bahá'u'lláh in Persia, and many others
still, are men like all the rest. They only stand out from the rest
because they have carried out God's will and purpose more faithfully
. . .[26]

In a letter addressed to Mrs Thornburgh-Cropper, an
American Bahá'í living in England, 'Abdu'l-Bahá again
mentions Tolstoy and the esteem which he has for him, while
wishing that he understood better the true meaning and the
global import of Bahá'u'lláh's message. 'Abdu'l-Bahá's Tablet
is the answer to a letter written by Mrs Thornburgh-Cropper,
in which she informs him that a certain John Kenworthy has
embraced the Cause and has the intention of visiting Count
Tolstoy:

There is an important matter in view, that is to teach the Cause to that
well-known personage, Tolstoy. For indeed his intentions are good
and his aim is service to the human world. Lately he hath become
somewhat disappointed and depressed because leaders of religion
have rejected him. Perhaps for this reason he may now have acquired
the capacity to respond to the influence of the Word of God.

If possible Mr Kenworthy should set out to visit him and speak to
him about the foundation of this great Cause. He should take the
translation of the 'Ishráqát' to him and explain that this divine Cause
is the fountainhead of great spirituality, and a wide portal leading to
the Glorious Kingdom. It is the source of the illumination of the
human world, and the cause of unity and harmony among all
nations. It is the foundation of universal peace and an edifice for
conciliation and well-being in this world. When this Cause is fully
established, it will completely remove every trace of discord and
enmity, will gather all the kindreds of this earth under the shadow of
one tent and make them live in unity. It will cause the east to befriend
the west, the north to fraternize with the south, and Turk to associate

with the Arab, the two hemispheres to be joined, and all countries and nations to become unified. These are the foundations of the Cause of God.[27]

A few days later Tolstoy received a letter from a Persian Bahá'í, P. Polisoídí. He was very happy about it and read the letter aloud before all the members of his family. This significant incident comes to us through his wife, Sophia A. Tolstaya,[28] and through his doctor, D.P. Makovitsky, who noted in his diary:

Leo Nicolaevich read aloud, even though the handwriting was very difficult to decipher, the letter received today from the Bahá'í, P. Polisoídí, from Rasht in Persia, in which he explains Bahá'u'lláh's teachings, and gives information about the spread and persecution of these teachings in Persia. Leo Nicolaevich was very pleased with the letter . . .[29]

Tolstoy replied to Polisoídí to express to him his gratitude in these terms: 'I thank you most heartily for the interesting and important information about the Bahá'ís. I will be very happy to be in touch with Dr Khan.'[30]

Youness Khan, mentioned by Tolstoy in the above letter, was a Persian Bahá'í who had been one of 'Abdu'l-Bahá's secretaries and who, a month later, sent Tolstoy a book about the life and teachings of 'Abdu'l-Bahá.[31]

The author was won over by reading this book, and on 22 February 1910 answered Youness Khan as follows: 'I am very grateful to you for the book about 'Abbás Effendi. I would like to take advantage of it to write a book for the general public about 'Abbás Effendi's beautiful teachings.'[32]

May we conclude from these statements by Tolstoy, which are so favourable to the Bahá'í Faith, that the author had accepted towards the end of his life these religious teachings? A testimony by Paul Biryukov could make us tend to reply affirmatively. Indeed, in his book *Tolstoï und der Orient* (Tolstoy and the Orient) Biryukov quotes the 'Journal' by Gusev, one of Tolstoy's secretaries, who, towards the end of 1909, noted the following incident:

Leo Nicolaevich related to a visitor: 'In Kazan there is God's Regiment, which is a Tartar Muslim sect. Their leader is Waissov from whom I received a letter yesterday. According to his opinion, his ideas have many points in common with my own, also with my concept of Christianity, and he wishes to come and see me. For me that's extremely interesting.

'One of his beliefs is that all men should share the same Faith. It's a Muslim sect. The other is known by the name of Bábísm. They are followers of Bahá'u'lláh who continued the Báb's work. To my great joy, a Bahá'í has paid me a visit. He wasn't very intelligent, but apart from that, I could have subscribed to his faith in all its aspects.'[33]

In spite of this statement Tolstoy never really accepted the Bahá'í Faith. There still remained one important point which prevented him from accepting this new religious message, and he says it himself in a letter to A. A. Kasimov, in which, while declaring himself in agreement with the basic principles of the Bahá'í Faith, he states that he does not believe in the infallibility of the divine messengers – a concept which, according to him, is one of the causes of division between men. This extremely clear letter is one of Tolstoy's last writings on this subject and, in my opinion, sums up very well the author's real position and true relationship to the Bahá'í Faith:

The answer to the first question is that there's no difference between the so-called prophets and wise men. Prophets specially sent by God never have existed and cannot exist. Attributing a prophetic mission peculiar to certain beings such as Moses, Christ, Krishna, Buddha, Muḥammad, Bahá'u'lláh as well as several others is one of the major causes of division and hatred between men.

So that is why attributing such a belief to certain people is something which is not pleasing to God and is a great sin. The words: 'I am the bread come down from heaven. He who eats this bread shall never die', and in general, the bread and the wine, as well as several similar passages from what people call the Sacred Scriptures, have no clear or important meaning, but are only comparisons, verbal embellishments, and sometimes simply nonsense. This is why we must understand and remind ourselves that what are called the Sacred Scriptures are a work written by human hands while men were immersed in all sorts of crass superstitions. Besides, these writings have been subjected to numerous translations and copies from which we should only take what agrees with sound reason and what is in harmony with the fundamentals of all religious teachings: Hindus, Chinese, Jews, Christians, Muslims and Bahá'ís, and we should reject all things which are not reasonable and which conflict with each other . . .

I know the Bahá'í teachings, and I am in agreement with its basic principles, except for the belief in the infallibility of its founders and a few other details.[34]

This non-belief in the infallibility of God's Messengers did not prevent Tolstoy from continuing to esteem the Bahá'í Faith increasingly. Makovitsky reports in his diary a conversation during which Tolstoy expressed very great admiration for Bahá'u'lláh's teachings. On 15 May 1910, a few months before his death, Tolstoy received a visit from Matveyev, a neighbour who had lived a long time in Persia. In noting the conversation which took place between them, Tolstoy's doctor relates that the Bábís were mentioned; and then, he writes, Matveyev commented that the Bahá'í movement was very interesting. To these words Tolstoy added the following: 'Very profound. I know of no other so profound.'[35]

Conclusion

Throughout this work, I have tried to uncover a little-known aspect of Tolstoy's thinking, but no less important for that, because the religious question became over the years Tolstoy's main preoccupation. His determination not to conform to established rules was immediately striking, as was his determination to remain open, without prejudice, to everything which could stir his imagination and curiosity. His spiritual development seemed to be that of a restless person, always in search of absolute truth.

Tolstoy's personality, simple and straightforward on first appearance, was much richer and more complex, and he had reached such a stage in his research that, in the end, he was convinced that he was both able and that he had a duty to communicate the results of his research to others.

His attitude towards the Bahá'í message was characterized by sudden changes of opinion, yet in his hesitations can be discerned a thirst to know ever more about the aims of this religious movement which on so many points confirmed the correctness of the ideas to which he had come.

At a time when the Bahá'í Faith was scarcely beginning to emerge from obscurity, and before it was really known in

Europe and on the other continents, Tolstoy had already shown an interest in it, and his interest increased the more he deepened his knowledge of its teachings.

Therein lies his greatest merit in this field. He was indeed ahead of his time.

Appendix

The Faith of Bahá'u'lláh

Extracts from a statement prepared for a United Nations Special Committee in 1947

by Shoghi Effendi

The Faith established by Bahá'u'lláh (1817–1892) was born in Persia about the middle of the nineteenth century and has, as a result of the successive banishments of its Founder, culminating in His exile to the Turkish penal colony of 'Akká, and His subsequent death and burial in its vicinity, fixed its permanent spiritual centre in the Holy Land, and is now in the process of laying the foundations of its world administrative centre in the city of Haifa.

Alike in the claims unequivocally asserted by its Author and the general character of the growth of the Bahá'í community in every continent of the globe, it can be regarded in no other light than a world religion, destined to evolve in the course of time into a world-embracing commonwealth, whose advent must signalize the Golden Age of mankind, the age in which the unity of the human race will have been unassailably established, its maturity attained, and its glorious destiny unfolded through the birth and efflorescence of a world-encompassing civilization.

Though sprung from Shí'ih Islám, and regarded, in the early stages of its development, by the followers of both the Muslim and Christian Faiths, as an obscure sect, an Asiatic cult or an offshoot of the Muḥammadan religion, this Faith is now increasingly demonstrating its right to be recognized, not as one more religious system superimposed on the conflicting creeds which for so many generations have divided mankind and darkened its fortunes, but rather as a restatement of the eternal verities underlying all the religions of the past, as a unifying force instilling into the adherents of these religions a new spiritual vigour, infusing them with a new hope and love for mankind, firing them with a new vision of the fundamental unity of their religious doctrines, and unfolding to their eyes the glorious destiny that awaits the human race.

The fundamental principle enunciated by Bahá'u'lláh, the followers of His Faith firmly believe, is that religious truth is not absolute but relative, that Divine Revelation is a continuous and progressive process, that all the great religions of the world are divine in origin, that their basic principles are in complete harmony, that their aims and purposes are one and the same, that their teachings are but facets of one truth, that their functions are complementary, that they differ only in the non-essential aspects of their doctrines, and that their missions represent successive stages in the spiritual evolution of human society.

The aim of Bahá'u'lláh, the Prophet of this new and great age which humanity has entered upon – He whose advent fulfils the prophecies of the Old and New Testaments as well as those of the Qur'án regarding the coming of the Promised One in the end of time, on the Day of Judgment – is not to destroy but to fulfil the Revelations of the past, to reconcile rather than accentuate the divergences of the conflicting creeds which disrupt present-day society.

His purpose, far from belittling the station of the Prophets gone before Him or of whittling down their teachings, is to restate the basic truths which these teachings enshrine in a manner that would conform to the needs, and be in consonance with the capacity, and be applicable to the problems, the ills and perplexities, of the age in which we live. His mission is to proclaim that the ages of infancy and of the childhood of the human race are past, that the convulsions associated with the present stage of its adolescence are slowly and painfully preparing it to attain the stage of manhood, and are heralding the approach of that Age of Ages when swords will be beaten into plowshares, when the Kingdom promised by Jesus Christ will have been established, and the peace of the planet definitely and permanently ensured. Nor does Bahá'u'lláh claim finality for His own Revelation, but rather stipulates that a fuller measure of the truth He has been commissioned by the Almighty to vouchsafe to humanity, at so critical a juncture in its fortunes, must needs be disclosed at future stages in the constant and limitless evolution of mankind.

The Bahá'í Faith upholds the unity of God, recognizes the unity of His Prophets, and inculcates the principle of the oneness and wholeness of the entire human race. It proclaims the necessity and the inevitability of the unification of mankind, asserts that it is gradually approaching, and claims that nothing short of the transmuting spirit of God, working through His chosen Mouthpiece in this day, can ultimately succeed in bringing it about. It, moreover, enjoins upon its followers the primary duty of an unfettered search after truth, condemns all manner of prejudice and superstition, declares the purpose of religion to be the promotion of amity and concord, proclaims its essential harmony with science, and recognizes it as the foremost agency for the pacification and the orderly progress of human society. It unequivocally maintains the principle of equal rights, opportunities and privileges for men and women, insists on compulsory education, eliminates extremes of poverty and wealth, abolishes the institution of priesthood, prohibits slavery, asceticism, mendicancy and monasticism, prescribes monogamy, discourages divorce, emphasizes the necessity of strict obedience to one's government, exalts any work performed in the spirit of service to the level of worship, urges either the creation or the selection of an auxiliary international language, and delineates the outlines of those institutions that must establish and perpetuate the general peace of mankind.

The Bahá'í Faith revolves around three central Figures, the first of whom was a youth, a native of Shíráz, named Mírzá 'Alí-Muḥammad, known as the Báb (Gate), who in May, 1844, at the age of twenty-five, advanced the claim of being the Herald Who, according to the sacred Scriptures of previous Dispensations, must needs announce and prepare the way for the advent of One greater than Himself . . .

Mírzá Ḥusayn-'Alí, surnamed Bahá'u'lláh (the Glory of God), a native of Mázindarán, Whose advent the Báb had foretold, was assailed by those same forces of ignorance and fanaticism, was imprisoned in Ṭihrán, was banished, in 1852, from His native land to Baghdád, and thence to Constantinople and Adrianople, and finally to the prison city of 'Akká, where He remained incarcerated for no less than twenty-four years, and in whose neighbourhood He passed away in 1892. In the course of His banishment, and particularly in Adrianople and 'Akká, He formulated the laws and ordinances of His Dispensation, expounded, in over a hundred volumes, the principles of His Faith, proclaimed His Message to the kings and rulers of both the East and the West, both Christian and Muslim, addressed the Pope, the Caliph of Islám, the Chief Magistrates of the Republics of the American continent, the entire Christian sacerdotal order, the leaders of Shí'ih and Sunní Islám, and the high priests of the Zoroastrian religion. In these writings He proclaimed His Revelation, summoned those whom He addressed to heed His call and espouse His Faith, warned them of the consequences of their refusal, and denounced, in some cases, their arrogance and tyranny.

His eldest son, 'Abbás Effendi, known as 'Abdu'l-Bahá (the Servant of Bahá), appointed by Him as His lawful sucessor and the authorized interpreter of His teachings, Who since early childhood had been closely associated with His Father, and shared His exile and tribulations, remained a prisoner until 1908, when, as a result of the Young Turk Revolution, He was released from His confinement. Establishing His residence in Haifa, He embarked soon after on His three-year journey to Egypt, Europe and North America, in the course of which He expounded before vast audiences, the teachings of His Father and predicted the approach of that catastrophe that was soon to befall mankind . . . In 1921 He passed away, and was buried in a vault in the mausoleum erected on Mount Carmel, at the express instruction of Bahá'u'lláh, for the remains of the Báb, which had previously been transferred from Tabríz to the Holy Land after having been preserved and concealed for no less than sixty years . . .

The Faith . . . is, it should be noted in this connection, essentially supernatural, supranational, entirely non-political, non-partisan, and diametrically opposed to any policy or school of thought that seeks to exalt any particular race, class or nation. It is free from any form of ecclesiasticism, has neither priesthood nor rituals, and is supported exclusively by voluntary contributions made by its avowed adherents. Though loyal to their respective governments, though imbued with the love of their own country, and anxious to promote, at all times, its best interests, the followers of the Bahá'í Faith, nevertheless, viewing mankind as one entity, and profoundly attached to its vital interests, will not hesitate to subordinate every particular interest, be it personal, regional or national, to the over-riding interests of the generality of mankind, knowing full well that in a world of interdependent peoples and nations the advantage of the part is best reached by the advantage of the whole, and that no lasting result can be achieved by any of the component parts if the general interests of the entity itself are neglected . . .

Bibliography

Works by Leo Tolstoy

The following are taken from *Polnoe Sobranie Sochinenii* (Complete Collected Works of L.N. Tolstoy). 90 Vols., Moscow: Gosudarstvennoe Izdatelstvo (State Editions), 1935–1958. For an English edition, consult *The Complete Works of Count Tolstoy*, trans. by L. Wiener, 24 Vols. (1904–1905), and *Tolstoy Centenary Edition*, trans. by L. and A. Maude, 21 Vols. (1928–1937).

'Dnevnik' (Diary). *P.S.S.* Vols. 52, 54 and 57.

'Ispoved' (Confession). *P.S.S.* Vol. 34 (1957), pp. 1–59.

'Kak i zachem zhit' (The How and Why of Living). *P.S.S.* Vol. 36 (1936), pp. 397–398.

'Otvet na opredelenie Sinoda ot 20–22 fevralya i na polucennye mnoyu po etomu sluchayu pisma' (Reply to the Synod on 20–22 February, and to the letter I received on that occasion). *P.S.S.* Vol. 34 (1957), pp. 245–253.

'O znachenii russkoy revolyutsii' (On the Significance of the Russian Revolution). *P.S.S.* Vol. 36 (1936), pp. 315–362.

'Patriotizm ili mir?' (Patriotism or Peace?) *P.S.S.* Vol. 90, pp. 45–53.

'Patriotizm i pravitelstvo' (Patriotism and Government). *P.S.S.* Vol. 90, pp. 425–453.

'Pisma' (Letters). *P.S.S.* Vols. 67, 72–76, and 78–81.

Quelle est ma Foi? (What Is My Faith?) Translated from the Russian by J. W. Bienstock. Paris: Delamain, Boutelleau et Cie., 1924.

La Vraie Vie (The True Life). Translated from the Russian by E. Halperin-Kaminsky. Paris: E. Fasquelle, 1901.

Studies on the Life, Work and Thought of Tolstoy

Biryukov, P. I. *Biographie de Tolstoï*. Berlin: J. P. Ladyznikov, 1921. 3 Vols.

Biryukov, P. I. *Tolstoï und der Orient*. Zürich and Leipzig: Rotapfel-Verlag, 1925.

Gusev, N. N. *Dva goda s L.N. Tolstym* (Two Years with L. N. Tolstoy). Moscow: Khudozhestvennaya literatura, 1973.

Makovitsky, D. P. *U Tolstogo: 1904–1910; 'Yasnopolyanskie zapiski'* (With Tolstoy: 1904–1910; 'Notes from Yasnaya Polyana'). Moscow: Nauka, 1979. 4 Vols.

Rolland, Romain. *La Vie de Tolstoï* (The Life of Tolstoy). Paris: Librairie Hachette, 1913.

Shifman, A. I. *Lev Tolstoy i vostok* (Leo Tolstoy and the Orient). Moscow: Nauka, 1971.

Tolstaya, S. A. *Dnevniki* (Diary). Moscow: Khudozhestvennaya literatura, 1978. 2 Vols.

Weisbein, Nicolas. *Tolstoï*. Paris: Presses Universitaires de France, 1968.

Zajdensnur, E. 'R. M. Rilke u Tolstogo' (R. M. Rilke with Tolstoy). In *Literaturnoe Nasledstvo*. Moscow: Izdatelstvo Akademii Nauk, 1939. Vol. 38, pp. 708–712.

Works by Bahá'u'lláh

Bahá'í Prayers. Wilmette, Illinois: Bahá'í Publishing Trust, 1982. (Includes prayers revealed by the Báb and 'Abdu'l-Bahá).

The Hidden Words. London: Bahá'í Publishing Trust, 1975.

Kitáb-i-Íqán. The Book of Certitude. Wilmette, Illinois: Bahá'í Publishing Trust, rev. edn. 1974.

The Proclamation of Bahá'u'lláh. Haifa: Bahá'í World Centre, 1972.

Tablets of Bahá'u'lláh. Haifa: Bahá'í World Centre, 1978.

Works by 'Abdu'l-Bahá

Selections from the Writings of 'Abdu'l-Bahá. Haifa: Bahá'í World Centre, 1978.

Works on the Bahá'í Faith

Bahá'í Studies. 'The Bahá'í Faith in Russia: Two Early Instances.' Thornhill, Ontario: Association for Bahá'í Studies, 1979. Vol. 5.

Balyuzi, H. M. *Edward Granville Browne and the Bahá'í Faith.* London: George Ronald, 1970.

Dreyfus, Hippolyte. *Essai sur le Bahá'ísme* (Essay on Bahá'ísm). Paris: Presses Universitaires de France, 3rd edn. 1962.

Esslemont, J. E. *Bahá'u'lláh and the New Era.* Wilmette, Illinois: Bahá'í Publishing Trust, 1980.

Gobineau, Arthur, Comte de. *Les Religions et les Philosophies de l'Asie Centrale* (The Religions and Philosophies of Central Asia). Paris, 1865.

Hatcher, W. S. and J. D. Martin. *The Bahá'í Faith.* New York: Harper and Row, 1985.

Huddleston, John. *The Earth is But One Country.* London: Bahá'í Publishing Trust, 1976.

New Encyclopaedia Britannica, The. Chicago: Encyclopaedia Britannica, Inc., 1983. Vol. 2, pp. 587–589 ('The Bahá'í Faith').

Nicolas, A.L.M. *Seyyed Ali Mohammed dit Le Bab* (Siyyid 'Alí Muḥammad, the Báb). Paris: Dujarric, 1905.

Shoghi Effendi. *God Passes By.* Wilmette, Illinois: Bahá'í Publishing Trust, rev. edn. 1979.

—————. *The World Order of Bahá'u'lláh.* Wilmette, Illinois: Bahá'í Publishing Trust, 2nd rev. edn. 1974.

Sulaymání, 'Azízu'lláh. *Masábíh-i-Hidáyat* (Biographies of some of the early Bahá'ís). Tehran: Bahá'í Publishing Committee, 1968.

Notes and References

1: TOLSTOY'S RELIGIOUS VISION

1 Introduction to *What Is My Faith?*
2 *Polnoe Sobranie Sochinenii*, vol. 46, p. 149.
3 *P.S.S.*, vol. 47, p. 12.
4 Ibid., p. 37.
5 Introduction to *The True Life*.
6 Ibid.
7 *The True Life*, Ch. XXXV.
8 Ibid.
9 *P.S.S.*, vol. 34, p. 245 (translated into French by Halperin-Kaminsky, in the preface to *The True Life*).
10 See Bibliography.
11 See Bibliography.
12 *P.S.S.*, vol. 54, p. 75.
13 *P.S.S.*, vols. 43 and 44.
14 *P.S.S.*, vol. 79, p. 142.
15 Preface to *The True Life*.
16 The relationship between Tolstoy and oriental religions has been the subject of several essays and commentaries. This aspect of Tolstoy's philosophy, which occupied an important place in the author's correspondence during the last years of his life, has been studied by many writers.

   Among the most exhaustive works, mention must be made of that of Paul Biryukov, who was both a friend and one of Tolstoy's secretaries: *Tolstoï und der Orient* (Tolstoy and the Orient), of which the following are the most important chapter headings:
   Chapter I: Tolstoy and the Indo-Brahmins;
   Chapter II: Tolstoy and the Indian Muslims;
   Chapter III: Tolstoy and the Persian, Egyptian and Turkish Muslims;

Chapter IV: Tolstoy and the Russian Muslims.
Another work devoted to the same subject is that of A. J. Shifman, *Lev Tolstoy i Vostok* (Leo Tolstoy and the Orient). Besides these, there are several other studies which deal with particular subjects, among which I will mention those of D. V. Belkin, 'L. N. Tolstoy i drevnie mysliteli Kitaya' (L.N. Tolstoy and the Ancient Thinkers of China), pp. 175–197; V. F. Bulgakov, *Knigi ob Indii biblioteke L. N. Tolstogo* (The Books on India in Tolstoy's Library), pp. 45–56; Z. M. Gildina, 'Lev Tolstoy i narody Indii' (Leo Tolstoy and the Peoples of India), pp. 307–36; L. Kim, *Lev Tolstoy v Japonii* (Leo Tolstoy in Japan), pp. 112–120; and V. S. Khramtsov, 'K Voprosu o Vliyanii filosofii L. N. Tolstogo na gandizm' (Concerning the Influence of Tolstoy's Philosophy on Gandhiism).

2: TOLSTOY AND THE BÁBÍ FAITH

1 *P.S.S.*, vol. 54, p. 121.
2 English in the text.
3 *P.S.S.*, vol. 67, p. 223.
4 See Bibliography.
5 Austrian author, born in Prague (1875–1926).
6 German orientalist and philosopher.
7 German author.
8 E. Zajdensnur, 'R. M. Rilke u Tolstogo', p. 708.
9 *P.S.S.*, vol. 72, p. 569.
10 Ibid., p. 117 (Letter to the editor of the newspaper, *New York World*).
11 P.S.S., vol. 73, p. 95 (original in French).

3: TOLSTOY AND THE BAHÁ'Í FAITH: FIRST CONTACTS

1 Paul Biryukov, *Tolstoï und der Orient*, p. 95.
2 *P.S.S.,* vol. 73, p. 109.
3 Shoghi Effendi, *The World Order of Bahá'u'lláh* (see Bibl.).
4 *P.S.S.*, vol. 69, p. 198.
5 *P.S.S.* vol. 54, p. 132.
6 Sulaymání notes: 'Jadhdháb here develops the history of the Báb and Bahá'u'lláh, of which mention in this book is unnecessary.'

7 Account taken from the book by 'Azízu'lláh Sulaymání, *Masábíh-i-Hidáyat* (see Bibliography).

4: AWARENESS OR CRITICISM?

1 *P.S.S.*, vol. 74, p. 207.
2 *P.S.S.*, vol. 75, p. 16 (original in English).
3 Ibid., p. 77 (original in French).
4 Ibid., p. 151 (footnote).
5 Ibid. (original in English).
6 Ibid., p. 91 (original in French).
7 D. P. Makovitsky, *U Tolstogo: 1904–1910; 'Yasnopolyanskie zapiski'*, vol. 1.
8 See Bibliography.
9 *P.S.S.*, vol. 41, p. 399 (Quotation is from *The Hidden Words* of Bahá'u'lláh, Arabic, No. 27).
10 Makovitsky, vol. 2, p. 90.
11 Russian translator of the works of H. George.
12 Makovitsky, vol. 2, p. 242.
13 *P.S.S.*, vol. 36, p. 361.
14 Ibid., pp. 397–398.
15 *P.S.S.*, vol. 76, p. 286.

5: ON THE THRESHOLD OF ACCEPTANCE?

1 *P.S.S.*, vol. 78, p. 306.
2 *P.S.S.*, vol. 80, p. 42 (original in French).
3 Makovitsky, vol. 4, p. 283.
4 *P.S.S.*, vol. 57, p. 18.
5 *P.S.S.*, vol. 79, p. 120.
6 Ibid.
7 Ibid., p. 193.
8 H. Dreyfus, *Essai sur le Bahá'ísme*, pp. 79–80.
9 *P.S.S.*, vol. 79, p. 131.
10 Ibid., p. 213.
11 Excerpt from Bahá'u'lláh's 'Tablet of Aḥmad', in *Bahá'í Prayers*, p. 212.
12 *P.S.S.*, vol. 79, p. 231.

13 'Abdu'l-Bahá, unpublished Tablet, translation authorized by the Universal House of Justice.

14 'Call to the Bahá'ís of the East and West', in *Selections from the Writings of 'Abdu'l-Bahá*, p. 283.

15 Russian name given by Tolstoy to Mírzá 'Alí-Akhbar Nakhjaváni, Mamed Khán being his father's first name.

16 *P.S.S.*, vol. 80, p. 102.

17 *P.S.S.,* vol. 79, p. 153.

18 Makovitsky, vol. 4, p. 79.

19 Bahá'u'lláh, 'Tablet of the Branch', cited in *The World Order of Bahá'u'lláh*, p. 135.

20 *P.S.S.*, vol. 80, p. 102.

21 Ibid., p. 138.

22 The 'Tablet of Splendours' ('Otblesky'), according to the note in *P.S.S.*, vol. 80, p. 219. This is Bahá'u'lláh's 'Ishráqát', published in *Tablets of Bahá'u'lláh*, pp. 101–134.

23 *P.S.S.*, vol. 80, p. 219.

24 *P.S.S.,* vol. 81, p. 106 (Tolstoy names his correspondent, Mamedkhanly, Turkish for the Russian word, Mamedkhanov).

25 Makovitsky, vol. 4, p. 113.

26 *P.S.S.,* vol. 81, p. 17.

27 'Abdu'l-Bahá, unpublished Tablet, translation authorized by the Universal House of Justice.

28 S. A. Tolstaya, *Dnevniki* (Diary), vol. 2, p. 30 (see Bibl.).

29 Makovitsky, vol. 4, p. 156.

30 *P.S.S.*, vol. 81, p. 48.

31 The book sent by Dr Y. Khan is that of M.H. Phelps, *Life and Teachings of Abbas Effendi: A Study of the Babis or Behais*, with an introduction by E. G. Browne, New York and London: G. P. Putnam's Sons, 1903.

32 *P.S.S.*, vol. 81, p. 107.

33 Biryukov, pp. 120–121.

34 *P.S.S.*, vol. 81, p. 77.

35 Makovitsky, vol. 4, p. 255.

Index

CPSIA information can be obtained at www.ICGtesting.com
Printed in the USA
LVOW040606020412

275661LV00001B/30/A

9 780853 982159